IN GRATITUDE

engrossing life, moving from social privilege to service of
rs, and played out against the tableau of enormous changes
ish society and the Catholic Church. Well worth the read.'
Casey, SJ, Director of the Diploma in Philosophy and Arts,
tifical University, Maynooth

ina Sculpture Garden in Glenmalure is the remarkable
ion of a remarkable woman, Catherine McCann. Many
ple have found sanctuary there, and one grim afternoon I
me one of them. As an agnostic, I was an unlikely visitor
itherine, a former nun, and her great friend, the equally
irkable Fr Charlie O'Connor, sj. But I was going through
kind of existential crisis, and in the context of the garden,
of their non-judgmental company, I found one of the first
ers of its resolution. I remain an agnostic, and very
y so, but I still return to Shekina for calm and good con-
on. Those who have wondered about the back story to
eation of Shekina, and to the extraordinary friendship
en McCann and O'Connor, will find a lucid and unusual
ive of our times in this revealing autobiography.'
ly Woodworth, ecologist, author and journalist

'Catherine McCann offers the reader a compassionate and unsen-
mental story of growing up in post-civil war Ireland, becoming
a novice in a great religious order, immersing herself in its mis-
io of charity, leaving after many years and reinventing herself
a new life without rancour or self-pity. A valuable window
into a recent past – courageous, poignant, enriching and honest.'
Margaret MacCurtain, historian

'Catherine's autobiography is a pleasure to read. It is written in an easy and riveting style which encourages the reader to want to turn over the pages. Her experience of Dublin in the 1930s to 50s is in itself an historical adventure. Here is a woman to whom nothing is impossible. Again and again she faces difficult personal decisions, making them with a courage and faith that is touching and edifying. Her journey through decades of change and loving friendships is insightful and inspiring. Thank you Catherine.'

Eric Guiry, former director of the Careers Advisory Service, Trinity College Dublin

IN GRATITUDE

The Story of a Gift-Filled Life

Catherine McCann

ORPEN PRESS

Published by
Orpen Press
Lonsdale House
Avoca Avenue
Blackrock
Co. Dublin
Ireland

email: info@orpenpress.com
www.orpenpress.com

Paperback ISBN 978-1-909895-76-8
ePub ISBN 978-1-909895-77-5
Kindle ISBN 978-1-909895-78-2
PDF ISBN 978-1-909895-79-9

Printed in Dublin by SPRINT-print Ltd.

To

everyone who has touched my life:

*family, friends, religious sisters, patients, clients,
workshop participants, fellow pilgrims,
visitors to Shekina, readers.*

Thank you

Foreword

Catherine McCann has led an unusual and varied life, and her memoirs reveal worlds of privilege and of spirituality that are foreign to many people's experience in twenty-first-century Ireland.

Her life has been characterised by a search for a closer relationship with God, an independence of mind, a positive approach to her many and varied undertakings, and – linked to this – a formidable energy.

The book, divided into three sections, reflects the three main phases of her life. She was the child of wealthy parents who as a girl led what she describes as a charmed existence. Her family lived in Simmonscourt, a 'big house' of the sort that often appears in works of fiction – but which is normally situated in rural Ireland rather than in the heart of what is now Dublin 4. There was a large number of staff both indoor and outdoor. She was shocked by the poverty she encountered when engaged in voluntary work for the Infant Aid Society.

From her First Holy Communion Catherine felt that God had come close to her. She became a nun, and for 25 years she was a member of the Sisters of Charity. Her experiences in the order were enriching as well as sometimes disillusioning; sisters' intellectual development was not encouraged and independent thought or action was largely frowned upon. She was taken aback by the two-tier system that demarcated nuns from lay sisters. Following her profession she trained and then worked as a physiotherapist.

Her life abroad, first as a student of theology in Rome and then as a teacher in Los Angeles, widened her horizons, after which she was summoned back to Ireland to continue her physiotherapy. More importantly, she commenced a close friendship with a Jesuit priest, Fr Charlie O'Connor. She regards this relationship of over 40 years as one of the greatest blessings of her life.

After 25 years as a nun, during a retreat Catherine received a 'call from God' which led to her departure from the Sisters of Charity. She then re-entered the lay world, but there was much continuity between her old and new existence – above all in her concern with deepening her spiritual life. She acquired the habit of reading newspapers and encountered other welcome features of the lay world. She continued her work as a physiotherapist and counsellor and ran workshops throughout Ireland. Her sculpture garden in Glenmalure took greater prominence as her sculpture collection grew and more people visited or spent a retreat day in the garden. Together with Charlie O'Connor she organised tours and pilgrimages to Israel–Palestine, Spain, Russia, Iona and elsewhere.

To her surprise she became a writer (this is her seventh book), she was awarded MA and PhD degrees (the latter involving a dissertation of 200,000 words), and the range of her interests spread ever more widely. In her energy and her spirituality she is a worthy descendant of some of the heroic Christian figures who have inspired her over many decades.

Michael Laffan
Professor Emeritus in History, University College Dublin

Contents

Introduction

For some years I have toyed with the idea of writing about my life. Such thoughts persisted, yet I failed to get started. The earlier period of my life left me fearful – fearful of it containing a bragging element. Recently, I see more clearly that this need not be so. Indeed, my early memories could contain a positive note in the sense of adding to Ireland's social history of a particular period, namely Dublin in the 1930s to 1950s. This awareness was heightened after viewing an illuminating documentary on the tenements.[1] In particular, this programme alerted me to aspects of life in Dublin city in post-Famine times. It noted that during that period, many of Dublin's more affluent citizens moved to newly developed suburbs, where there was more land. My grandfather was born just before the Famine and came to reside in 'the big house' in Ballsbridge in the last quarter of the nineteenth century.

The longer I live, the more I see the importance of context when trying to understand human experience. Context has to do with places as well as historical periods. A more accurate knowledge of history enlarges our understanding of the present. Learning to see how reality was perceived over different periods of history and then noticing how viewpoints evolve over time gives us a broader perspective on present views, attitudes and situations. Places and times have a strong influence on everyone,

---

[1] *The Tenements*, broadcast on TV3 in August 2011.

even if this is not always recognised. Our core belief systems also influence our lives, more than we realise or admit.

I delayed starting my story partly because it involved a change from my previous books, in which I wrote about issues in relation to social, emotional and spiritual care. In both *Who Cares? A Guide for All Who Care for Others* and *Falling in Love with Life: An Understanding of Ageing* I took an entirely objective approach to these topics. In *Diary of a Hippy: Journeying through Surgery* and in a chapter of *Saying Yes to Life: A Way to Wisdom*, I was somewhat more personal.

This book has no specific audience. As I write, who it is for is less clear. Still, a certain impetus urges me to share with others the many opportunities that were open to me and the gifted life I have experienced. Such happenings and my reflections on these inevitably mean that the pronouns 'I' and 'my' are to the fore. Having recently completed doctoral studies where facts had to be substantiated, this work has only personal authenticity to rely on. I realise that if this writing is to come across as genuine, honesty is essential. I endeavour not to embellish but to be as accurate as my memory allows.

What I write largely emerges as I write. For example, what I wrote yesterday would be different to what I would write today. I know I am not a 'word' person in the sense that I am no good at Scrabble or crosswords and also I am aware of my limited knowledge of grammar and sentence construction. I would say I write as I talk. I do realise reworking is necessary so that the text is clear and, even more important, that it sincerely expresses reality as close to the truth as I perceive it to be from this present stage of my life. A recent *Irish Times* piece articulated well a writing style similar to my own where an author suggests real writing gets done when self-consciousness drops off – 'When I'm thinking as I write, those are the pages that get thrown away .... It's like prayer or like exercise: you work towards this spot, which is beyond the work, where there's freedom or transcendence ... *writing happens in the moment*.'[2]

---

[2] *Irish Times*, 19 September 2012, 'If I Think as I Write, Those Pages Are Thrown Away', Belinda McKeon writing about the author Nathan Englander. (Italics mine.)

A final and continued hesitancy comes from the present limitations of my memory. I can only contribute what I remember and so there will be gaps all through. I am also keenly aware that I can only offer my own perspective. Everyone's experience is unique and so, for example, in Part One, my siblings' experiences will inevitably differ from mine. Suddenly, however, getting started became easy. My sister Bridget gave all us siblings a notebook for Christmas 2011, asking us to jot down any memories we had of Simmonscourt – the name of the big house. That was the trigger and I was off on this journey within days.

I am now in my eightieth year and, as I look back, I see my life falling into three distinct periods. The first (and presumably the most formative) is the first nineteen years, when I lived in the big house, from early memories up to my father's death. The second covers the time spent as a religious sister and my professional career. Part Three focuses on the period after leaving religious life, which includes the remainder of my working life, the time after leaving formal work and finally my present life.

Part One

LIVING IN THE BIG HOUSE

The Household

Part One – A Brief History

Simmonscourt was not only a 'big house' but also had so much land around it, and yet it was only two miles from Dublin city centre. The official title was Simmonscourt Castle and it was commonly known by that name by locals, friends and the postal services. The house itself was not a castle. Rather there was, and still is, the ruins of a tower or gateway to the original castle in the grounds near the house:[1]

> Simmonscourt was formerly called Smothescourt, which name was derived from the Smothe family, who in the fourteenth century occupied the estate known as the 'forty acres' situated on the northwestern boundary of the district of Merrion …. The Castle, of which a gateway still survives, was probably built by Thomas Smothe, who held the office of Remembrancer of the Exchequer in the reign of Edward the Third. It was evidently a considerable structure.[2]

---

[1] The Phoenix Park Visitors' Centre has a room in the Ashtown Castle section that lists the castles around Dublin and 'Simons Court' tower, as Simmonscourt was then known, is included.

[2] This quotation is taken from a history found in the preface of *Simmonscourt Castle 1780–1936*. The source is unknown. The book also offers identical photographic

Simmonscourt appears to have been used over several centuries by ecclesiastics; firstly by the Priory of All Hallowes and then the Priory of Holy Trinity, and later by its successor, the Cathedral of Christ Church. At the end of the seventeenth century, the castle lay in ruins until the beginning of the eighteenth century, when a house was built. A hundred years later, my grandfather bought the property in the mid-1870s, most likely in its earlier Victorian form.

The property in our time was a square-shaped site[3] from which a small section was donated by my grandmother to the Poor Clares in the early 1900s. Our section comprised 18.5 acres.[4] Its boundaries were Simmonscourt Road to the north, the Masonic School (now Bewley's Hotel) and some back gardens of Merrion Road houses to the east, to the south the back gardens of many Shrewsbury Road houses, and to the west the grounds of Anglesea football club and other back gardens of houses on Anglesea Road. There were two entrances, the main one on Simmonscourt Road and the other through what we termed 'the lane', now officially called Simmonscourt Lane.

Part Two – The Family

My paternal grandparents were James McCann (1840–1904) and Mary O'Hagan (d.1936). My grandmother died when I was two. I used to think that I remembered Gaga, as she was known, but I was probably recalling a large photo of her that was in the house. The fact that talk about her lingered for some years made her seem very real and we often referred to 'Gaga's room'. She seems to have been both kind and formidable. Her generosity was manifested in her giving away part of the estate to establish a Poor Clare convent at Simmonscourt (more on

---

views that compare the exterior and interior of some rooms and their furnishings as it was in the early Victorian period and then as we knew it.

[3] See outline drawings, descriptions and comments on the premises and interior of the house in Appendices I and II. The drawings are done from memory so proportions may not be strictly accurate. Obviously in connection with the grounds there were no straight lines as portrayed in this sketch.

[4] The grounds of Simmonscourt comprised 178 acres in 1660.

that later). She also became well known as a contributor to many charitable organisations, frequently in association with the Archbishop of Dublin, William Walsh,[5] with whom she was friendly. She married James McCann in 1872 in St Kevin's Church, Harrington Street, Dublin. The marriage certificate states that her father, Arthur O'Hagan, was a solicitor and the family lived in 9 Harcourt Street, Dublin.[6] They had six children: May (1873–1920), who entered the Poor Clares in 1898; Jim (1875–1951), who became a Jesuit; Thomas (b.1877), who died from bronchitis when one month old; Arthur (b.1878), who became a Navan farmer and married Aunt Louis; and my father, John (1880–1952).

There is considerable information about my paternal grandfather, since he was quite a public figure. He was described as a 'homely and hearty character … good company … delighted in hospitality and laughter' and that 'McCann's table was ever open.'[7] He was a spiritual man, reading a chapter of the *Imitation of Christ* each morning before setting out for work. He is also known to have written prayers.[8] His contribution to society was varied, from banking, to stockbroking, to farming and, in the last four years his life, to parlimantarian. De Blacam's ten-page article on my grandfather, written forty years after his death, spelled out in detail his 'noteworthy contribution to history'.[9] This article left me with feelings of pride that my grandfather

---

[5] William Walsh, Archbishop of Dublin 1885–1921. A note on the diocesan website says he was 'sympathetic to Irish Nationalism and advocated Home Rule and agrarian land reform'.

[6] Arthur O'Hagan Solicitors was one of the oldest established solicitor firms based in Dublin, being originally set up in 1852. The Arthur O'Hagan website displayed a photograph of their offices at 9 Harcourt Street, the house where my grandmother lived. However in 2006 O'Hagan Solicitors merged with Mason, Hayes & Curran and two years later the O'Hagan name was dropped.

[7] Aodh de Blacam, 'James McCann, 1840–1904: A Pioneer of Rural Restoration', *Studies: An Irish Quarterly Review*, Vol. 34, No. 133 (March 1945), p. 99.

[8] de Blacam, p. 100. This author even quotes two of his prayers. In addition to de Blacam I also gathered some information about my grandfather from the Navan Historical Society website (www.navanhistory.ie), and also from Donnybrook local historian Danny Parkinson.

[9] de Blacam, p. 95.

had been such a great pioneer and reformer. He showed a passion for justice, particularly for those working on the land.

He was born in Channon Rock,[10] the second child of four sons and five daughters of James McCann and Dorothy Hickey, both of County Louth. It was a Gaelic-speaking area and the McCanns were one of the oldest and most respected clans in the area. James, my grandfather, was brought up among tillage farmers and millers and never lost his love of farming. He could have been related to John McCann of McCann and Hill Ltd, famous millers in Drogheda at the time.[11] He was educated by the Christian Brothers in Drogheda then for a brief period became a clerk at the Drogheda Steam Packet Company. At eighteen he worked in the Hibernian Bank in College Green and stayed there for ten years. He then left banking and became a stockbroker and subsequently opened his own firm on Anglesea Street, next door to the Stock Exchange. He married Mary O'Hagan in 1872. From their marriage certificate, I discovered he was a widower when he married my grandmother, something we, his grandchildren, knew nothing about.

It seems from a history written by Fr Crean[12] about the Sacred Heart parish in Donnybrook that my grandfather bought Simmonscourt Castle in 1878.[13] Where he lived in Dublin for the previous twenty years is not clear. His marriage certificate gave his residence as the St Stephen's Green Club. May, his first

---

[10] Channon Rock was a townsland in the parish of Louth and the diocese of Armagh near the Ulster border.

[11] John Holohan, historian and member of the Irish Georgian Society, showed me a miller's sack with the name 'McCann and Miller' printed on it and the words, 'The famous Drogheda Oatmeal, *Mother's Pride*.' It would seem that this was John McCann, who built a mill at Beamond, four miles from Drogheda, in 1800. This oatmeal business flourished until 1964, when the business was taken over by Odlums.

[12] Fr Crean was parish priest of Donnybrook and wrote a history of the Poor Clares in 1966. This date was also affirmed in de Blacam's article.

[13] It was not possible to trace dates of his coming to live in Simmonscourt in the Registry of Deeds other than that the property was recorded under St Mary's parish, Donnybrook. Registration was not compulsory in those days. The Valuation Office did register the property under James McCann in Dublin City Council, Pembroke East, in the years 1896–1899. After his death the name changed to Mary O'Hagan (my grandmother) and in 1913 to my father, John McCann.

child, was born in Bray and he was friendly with the parish priest there, Fr James Healy – factors which indicate he possibly lived in Bray after his marriage.

From the 1890s, according to de Blacam, he began to devote his energies to the revival of rural life. He appears to have done well as an stockbroker and sold shares to buy properties in Navan itself and a considerable amount of land in Telltown and other surrounding areas, including a second home, Ardsallagh House. He developed schemes to help workers in the Boyne valley, including dividing his estate into smaller farms and building cottages, with proper water supply and other facilities, termed 'McCann holdings', which later passed into the ownership of those who lived in them. One of his greatest legacies seems to have been his promotion of tillage farming. In addition, he opened rural industries: a bacon curing factory and sawmills, as well as a furniture factory, the latter leading to Navan's prosperity in the furniture trade. He reopened a water route to Drogheda, even bought ships, and established a dockyard in Navan. Other projects included becoming chairman of the Grand Canal Company and founding a local newspaper, the *Irish Peasant*.

De Blacam summarised my grandfather's rural endeavours as follows: 'James McCann was not content to live in the city writing articles on how the countryside should be led. He had the tradition of country life in his bones and happily possessed the means to follow out his ideal. That is to say, he went to the countryside, lived and worked it, and taught by his acts. He gave the countryside what it needs most of all, personal local leadership. He taught small men in leading them, and he taught men of substance by his example.'[14]

In the 1890s, it remains unclear whether the firm of James McCann and Son Stockbrokers, which continued until after my father's death, was still run by my grandfather as well as his managing all his endeavours in Co. Meath, or whether he relied on his son Jim and later John, my father. The firm was formally

---

[14] de Blacam, p. 102.

taken over by a son in 1902, presumably my father, as Jim had entered the Jesuits in his mid-twenties.

From 1900 until his death in 1904, he was a Member of Parliament as an independent nationalist for the St Stephen's Green division. In 1901, he spoke in parliament about the extremely high cost of transporting agricultural products in Ireland as being the highest in the world. He advocated that railways and canals should be unified as a national service, nationally owned and controlled.

He died on 16 February 1904 in Simmonscourt in a matter of days, from being perfectly healthy to developing a fatal bout of pneumonia.[15]

The *Meath Chronicle* wrote: 'The townspeople [of Navan] of every rank are united in deploring the loss of one who by his benevolence and public spirit had conferred upon them substantial and lasting benefits.' They further showed their appreciation of his generosity at his death by ordering a special train to take 700 of them to Glasnevin Cemetery for his burial.[16] The Cardinal Archbishop of Armagh and the Archbishop of Dublin also attended, indicating the esteem in which he was held.

A lengthy obituary in the *Irish Times* written in February 1904 states, 'there were few better known or more respected citizens' and goes on to mention, among his other accolades, his being a member of the Dublin Stock Exchange, a Justice for the Peace in the counties of Dublin and Meath, a member of the Pembroke Urban Council, chairman of the Irish Church Property Company, and a member of several other public boards. 'He took a very warm interest in the revival of old, and the developing of new, industries …. The betterment of his fellow countrymen was his sincerest wish. Dublin has lost a very eminent citizen and the country at large a true friend.'

---

[15] The Glasnevin Trust records state his death was due to heart failure.
[16] My grandfather is buried in vault 47 in the O'Connell section of Glasnevin Cemetery. Since his infant son is buried there it can be presumed he purchased the vault in that year (1877). It now contains the remains of seven members of the family: my grandfather and his infant son Thomas; my father; his first wife, Jane, and their infant son Seán; and my mother.

Our father, John, commonly known as Jack, born in 1880, was the youngest in that family. He was sent away to Beaumont, a Jesuit boarding school near London, but apart from that we have no further information about his earlier years. My father and his older brother Arthur would have been the two inheritors of my grandfather's estate, since their two other siblings had entered religious life. Presumably Arthur decided he wanted to live the life of a farmer and so settled at Ardsallagh House, thus paving the way for my father to take over as the master in Simmonscourt. He must have had to make space for his mother for the remaining 32 years of her life. For how long after her husband died Gaga remained mistress of the house is not known; most likely until my father married.

Like his father, my father married twice. His first wife was Jane Dillon (d.1926) and they had six children, our half-brothers and sisters. They are now all dead. Jim, the eldest, became a Benedictine monk at Downside, taking the name of Dom Cuthbert. Peggy (d.1962) married Cecil Martin[17] and they had three children, Anthony, Robin and Susan. Bobby died of diabetes in his early twenties, probably in 1936, two years after my birth; I know he was at my christening. Paddy, who never married, became a stockbroker and took over my father's stockbroking business when he died. Mary (d. 2005) married David O'Neill and they had two children, Simon and Jane. David's job as a pilot led to this family living for several years in Aden and then later in England. Seán died as an infant of seven months in 1911. Five years after my father's first wife died of cancer he remarried, and then the second family appeared. Thankfully all five of us are alive and well: John, myself, Elizabeth, Bridget and Monica.

---

[17] Cecil's family owned T & C Martin, a big builders' provider. Mary, his sister, founded the Medical Missionaries of Mary. Their mother, Mary, a widow and mother of twelve, wrote a diary following the news of her son Charlie going missing during the war in January 1916, concluding with his death in March. This diary went online in 2012, having been researched by Trinity College Dublin and University College Cork. The database was launched by the Minister for the Arts, Heritage and the Gaeltacht, Jimmy Denihan, 'as a rich source for anyone interested in Irish history'. See *Irish Times*, 3 October 2012.

My father carried on in the footsteps of his father, settling into a stockbroking career and becoming president of the Irish Stock Exchange in 1916, 1917 and 1923. I have never been quite sure whether stockbroking is a profession or a business. I have the same query about accountancy. Like his father, he also, over the years, became either chairman or member of several public boards. These included the Grand Canal Company, Irish Rail, the Tram Company, Irish Cinemas, the Irish Sugar Company, the Irish Gas Company and the Royal Bank.[18]

Apart from work, my father was an accomplished sportsman, whose greatest claim to fame was winning an Olympic silver medal for polo in London in 1908. He played golf and tennis but his main interest was horses and especially hunting with the Ward Union Hunt or the Meath Harriers polo, and later breeding and owning racehorses. Shooting was a less frequent pastime. He was a keen supporter and president for some years of the Fitzwilliam Lawn Tennis Club. He was also a keen weather watcher, and every morning a gardener would come in with a book in which were recorded the previous day's rainfall and temperature, which he would study during breakfast before leaving for office. Each evening, on arriving home, he and my mother would change into formal evening wear for dinner. At weekends, when not at his sporting activities, he would be at home but he largely remained a remote figure to us as children. He could, I sense, be stern but I think fair. What I do recall was that he encouraged us to invite our friends to the house, both informally and for parties. He showed an interest in our sporting pursuits, especially tennis.

He had a verse that he often recited for us, which he thought contained wise advice and which he presumably tried to put into practice himself:

---

18 This bank amalgamated with two other banks to form Allied Irish Banks in 1966. The Foster's Place branch of the Royal Bank was used by both my parents and later myself. Today this listed building is owned by Trinity College and the old mahogany counters over which the public did their business are still *in situ*. I recall, from my childhood days, going there with my mother and not being tall enough to look over those massive structures.

When you've got a job to do, do it now;
If it's one you wished was through, do it now;
If you're sure the job's your own, just tackle it alone;
Don't hem or haw or groan. Do it now.

Like his father before him, my father had a social conscience, although how much he carried forward his father's projects, and how entrepreneurial and philanthropic he was, remains unclear. He did do some work with the Society of St Vincent de Paul. My half-brother Paddy said he tried often, in my father's later years, to get him to divide up the estate so as to avoid death duties, which were very high at the time, but he refused. It would be interesting to know his reasons – was it that he wished to be and remain a conscientious citizen? He had a deep religious faith. An example of his personal devotion was revealed years later by Mother Canisius, who worked in the old St Vincent's Hospital in St Stephen's Green. She said he often called into the convent chapel to say his rosary on the way home from work. I presume he kept a financial eye on the Poor Clares during and after the death of first his sister and later his mother.

He was hunting into the last year of his life and had several accidents, the last of which he never really recovered from. He died suddenly, dropping dead in his bedroom on 24 August 1952 as the result of a heart attack. His funeral occurred during a newspaper strike but the word got around and a sizeable number turned up at his funeral Mass. My mother and the four of us girls did not go to the cemetery, which appears to have been part of the culture at the time.

***

My maternal grandparents were Louis-Henri de Laubenque (1867–1928) and Josephine Esther Meagher (1867–1926). Sadly, I know little about them. Records going back to 1530[19] showed that my grandfather was a descendant of the French Gaillard

[19] A cousin of my mother's found some records in the British Museum.

de Laubenque family, whose origins were in Normandy. One branch of the family sadly came to an end when its last member was guillotined. Another branch moved to Toulouse and then, in the late 1700s, settled in Martinique, possibly fleeing the onset of the French Revolution. My grandfather was born in St Lucia,[20] a fact verified by our Uncle Henry, who traced his baptismal record to that country. In 1898, my grandfather married Josephine (daughter of James Joseph Meagher, of Irish descent) in Castries, the capital of St Lucia; where they met we do not know and we have no further information on Josephine.

Our mother, Madeleine (1901–1987), and her three brothers, Leon (b.1898), Henry (b.1900) and Bernard (b.1903), were all born in Assam in India, where my grandfather worked as an accountant for a number of tea plantations. My mother rarely talked about her parents or her early life. I never had any 'feel' for my grandfather's personality but one thing I do record my mother saying about her mother was how unbearable she found living through the hot season in India. She felt that her mother probably suffered from depression. What a deprivation it must have been for her to see so little of her children when they went away to England for their entire schooling period. She also said she thought her mother's family originally came from Tipperary. My grandmother became ill on the journey home from India when returning to the UK upon her husband's retirement and they stopped for her to recuperate in Paris. Sadly she died there and was buried in Père Lachaise Cemetery. I visited her grave once when I was seventeen.

We only know snippets about our mother's earlier years. She and her brothers were sent from India to England for their schooling, she being the second youngest and going at the early age of eight to a convent school in the south of England. For secondary school, she went to the Holy Child Convent in Mayfield, Sussex, a school which I subsequently attended. The four of them never went home to India for holidays because the

---

[20] My great-grandfather Charles, a French nobleman, seems to have been the first Gaillard de Laubenque to settle in St Lucia, the West Indian island next to Martinique.

length of time to travel from India to the UK and back was just too long, so my mother saw little, if any, of her parents over a period of ten years. On leaving school, she returned to India; Leon went to work in Paris, where he spent the rest of his life; Henry entered a seminary in England and was ordained in 1926, living the last twenty years of his priestly ministry as parish priest of Canterbury; and Bernard settled in London, where he took up insurance work. None of her brothers married, nor did our father's three siblings, so, somewhat surprisingly, we have no first cousins.

My mother joined her parents on their retirement journey back to England, during which her mother died in Paris, and on returning to England she looked after her father until his death. Within a couple of years, she was introduced to my father by one of her school friends from Mayfield. A romance started and they soon married. It was a quiet wedding in the Spanish Place church in London on 25 November 1931. She then came and took up residence in Simmonscourt. It must have been difficult to find herself the mistress of such a big household and perhaps even more difficult was the fact that she had no friends here and my father's friends would have been older than her and had different backgrounds and interests. For some unknown reason, my father's pet name for my mother was Midge. (None of us had pet names except Elizabeth, whom my father called Libby – he insisted at birth that all of us have only one first name.)

Managing the household and rearing the five of us became my mother's full-time occupation. She initiated, or became involved, in most things we did, and was interested in our activities, an interest that she later extended to her grandchildren. I sense she found some of the job difficult, such as entertaining, as well as managing the staff and seeing to their well-being. She played golf in her earlier married life, but her real hobby, and something she was very good at, was needlework – sewing, knitting, embroidery and especially cross-stitching. To this day, we treasure the various dolls' clothes she made, some of which have now been passed on to her great-granddaughters. Some of her voluntary work consisted in helping out at St Brigid's Nursery School in Mountjoy Square and being involved in a weekly Apostolic Guild meeting where she and the other women made vestments and clothes for children in the missions. She dressed with an elegant simplicity and was careful, in a non-fussy way, to look after her appearance. She was a warm, hospitable, kind yet rather reticent person, never imposing her views on anyone. Her religious faith was very real, even if quietly expressed. From my earliest memory and through most of her life she had Thomas à Kempis' *The Imitation of Christ* at her bedside, aiming to read a section of it each night.

I never sensed tension between my parents. I recall a friend of mine, Marie, asking my mother, then in her early eighties, what their relationship was like. She replied, 'He was always respectful of me and always kind.' I was never aware of either parent being rude or abrasive with the servants or other staff.

Part Two – The Staff

Another important part of the household was the servants and staff. 'Servant' was the name given to those who worked indoors and 'staff' to those who did outdoor work. All the servants lived in, with the exception of the butler, who resided with his family in the back lodge. Over the years, we had a total of eight indoor servants and seven outdoor staff. They included a butler, a parlour maid, two housemaids, a cook, a kitchen maid, a nanny and a nursery maid. They all wore uniforms, but different categories had different outfits, with, for example, one for the parlour maid and another for the housemaids. We called them by their first names except the butler who was known by his surname, and the cook, who had the title 'Mrs'. In turn, they called us Miss or Master and then our first name. Hence I was always called 'Miss Catherine' and my brother 'Master John'. My parents were simply referred to as 'the Master' or 'the Mistress'. All the servants had one full day off in the week.

Kelly (Mathew), the butler, is certainly the one we all remember most. He was a kind, gentle and most patient man. He was very good to my father and looked after many of his needs, taking charge of his dressing room and all his clothing. As well as really being my father's valet, he also had his butler duties, like seeing that all was in order for the meals, and then serving. He also looked after the wine cellar and cleaned all our shoes. He was the general overseer who ensured that everything functioned well.

Mary (Sweeney), the parlour maid, was the oldest of the staff. Mary set the table for meals, served and did all the washing up in her pantry. She also helped with the silver cleaning and took care of all the china and glassware. The housemaids seemed to change more frequently than the rest of the staff and, as a consequence, I cannot recall any of their names. Their duties were cleaning the house, making the beds, collecting the slops, turning down the beds in the evening, lighting the fires and looking after the laundry.

The cook's name was Mrs Dixon, and she was followed later by a Mrs Dawson. She cooked all the meals for the family, and for the servants and some staff. My mother met her every morning to discuss meals and to give out materials needed from the store room. I cannot recall who ordered the food from the butcher, fishmonger or general grocery store but it was all delivered to the house that day. Kitchen maids helped with the preparation of the food, especially the fruit and vegetables, and did the constant washing up in their scullery. Either the cook or kitchen maid used to feed the hens and collect the eggs.

Nanny's role (Margaret Kelly) was, to my eyes, very different. She called us by our names and, in many respects, really played a mother's role. She slept with the two youngest and when a new arrival came, the eldest moved out into a room of his or her own. She helped dress and bath us, made our breakfast, took us out for walks, got us ready for our lessons, said our night prayers with us and put us to bed. I remember having a crisis when I was not sure who I loved more, my mother or my nanny; I felt it was Nanny, while sensing that this was not quite right. We also had a nursery maid for a short while, when the fourth child, Bridget, arrived.

As I look back, I have feelings of sadness and shame about how little we knew of the personal lives of all these people. Apart from Kelly, who lived in the lodge and had young children, so there was some contact there, we knew nothing about the others. We never asked and nothing was ever said. Even though I met Nanny on occasions after we had all dispersed, I do not recall hearing of her death. The staff never spoke about their personal lives, and we never knew where they came from, Dublin or the country, or what they did on their days off.

Our governess, Maud Brennan, whom I discovered later was an aunt of Joan FitzGerald, Garret FitzGerald's wife, came every morning for three hours. She began with my brother, John, and then a year later with myself. More about our lessons will be discussed in the next chapter. A clock man came every week to check and wind all the clocks in the house. My father had a thing about time and every clock was set five minutes fast. A dressmaker, Annie Dunne, came when she was needed, which was usually to make dresses for special occasions for us children. I appreciated this more in my mid-teens when she came to make evening dresses for me for the various parties I went to.

The outdoor staff comprised seven people: the head gardener and three other gardeners, a cow man, a groom and a chauffeur. The head gardener, Fitzpatrick, lived with his family in the front lodge, and was overseer of all the work the other gardeners did. I recall him mainly in the greenhouses with new seedlings or cuttings, or attending to the soft fruits in the walled garden. Two of the other gardeners were called Larry and Harry. There was much to be done: cutting the grass on the extensive lawns, attending to fruit trees and fruit picking, planting, pruning, weeding, and planting and caring for vegetables and bringing these to the kitchen as required. I remember one particular event: my father was very proud of the two grass tennis courts, and at certain times of the year the grass was rolled over by a big roller pulled by a horse, for which the animal wore special shoes.

The cow man obviously looked after and milked the cows and separated the milk. He also looked after the pigs when we had them. The groom, Curley, cared for the horses and helped to exercise them. O'Toole, the chauffer, must have come immediately after the war ended in 1945. He was followed by Kinch. They kept the cars in good trim as well as driving us around, although this didn't happen all that often, since we normally used the bus or tram to go to town or swimming and so on.

Looking back, I see that Simmonscourt offered employment to several people. You could have viewed it as an enterprise or as a type of community. From our perspective, there were always people around, and everyone involved was somehow making the enterprise work, or alternatively, was by their contributions keeping the community functioning and alive.

2

Earliest Memories to My Eleventh Year

My mother recorded the following facts in my baby book. I was born at 3 a.m. on 21 June 1934 in the Leinster Nursing Home in Dublin. The doctor attending was Paul Carton and the nurse was Winifred Bruton. The usual details about my first steps, etc., were mentioned, as was the fact that my first pet was a Pekinese dog called Dopey. She ended by describing me as 'a very fat baby'.

I was baptised on 27 June at the Sacred Heart Church, Donnybrook, by Monsignor Molony, the parish priest. My mother, as was customary, was not present because she was still in the nursing home. Those who did attend were: my father, my brother, John, Gaga, Paddy, Peggy and Bobby (my half-brothers and sister), Nanny, and four names I no longer recognise. My godfather, Uncle Bernard, was not there. He gave me the gift of an insurance policy, which still lies with the insurance company as I have no way of claiming it since the company's name is unknown. Pity! I no longer remember who my godmother was. I had two guests at my first birthday party: Joan and Alan O'Grady. The O'Grady family did play an important part in the lives of all of us siblings. I did not realise this relationship went so far back. Nanny McCann and Nanny O'Grady were friends, and they in turn introduced the two mothers to each other. The latter became firm friends. Another family listed early on were the Collins. We have kept contact with these families to the present day.

In 1939, when I was five, I began lessons with Miss Brennan and stayed with her until I was ten. I recall the first lesson, when she started off with John and I playing pelmanism[21] and I won. I was taught to read and write and the usual basic subjects: maths, history, geography. I learned enough so that when I went to school as a day girl to Loreto in Foxrock at the age of eleven, I was on par with the other girls in my class. Lessons were not a bore; however neither do I recall finding them exciting. My brother was sent to school earlier at the age of eight. He went on his bike to Xavier's on Morehampton Road, a private school, whose headmaster was Mr Hughes. While there, John made several lifelong friends, particularly his friend Dermot. My sisters after me stayed with Miss Brennan until they were eight, at which age they went to the primary school in Killiney which, in Elizabeth's case, had just opened.

When war broke out between Britain and Germany that September of 1939, my main concern was that Nanny, who was on holidays in Liverpool, might not be able to get home. I can vividly recall my strong feelings of anxiety about this happening. Thankfully, she did return safely.

The war formed a backdrop to my early years. John had big maps in his room and lots of drawing pins, with which he outlined where the troops were and how they were advancing. Apart from having no cars and hearing some upsetting stories, our lives were not noticeably different. We did eat a lot of rabbit stew but were lucky to have meat every day. There were, of course, plenty of fruit and vegetables to be had from the garden and always fresh milk, cream and homemade butter. An air-raid shelter was built in the front shrubbery, which, fortunately, never had to be used. After the war, it became a store house for apples and pears. Everyone in the household was fitted with gas masks.

---

[21] This is a card game where a pack of cards is spread over the table face down. You turn up a card and then try to find a match of this card, e.g., a queen or a five, and the person who has matched most pairs at the end of the game is the winner.

In the earlier years, we took most meals in the nursery. I can still picture that room: the fireplace with a fender around it, a gas ring for making the groats or porridge, the press where the toys were kept, the table used for meals and lessons, an armchair in one corner for Nanny and, at one stage, a high table for my canary's cage. Nanny would take us for walks, mainly to Herbert Park, usually going via Anglesea Road. I knew every crevice in the stones on the wall along the Dodder and used to be fascinated by the moss and other vegetation that hid there – the beginning of micro awareness? The going-to-bed ritual of bathing and being taught and saying prayers at Nanny's knee, leaving our shoes out to be cleaned, and saying goodnight to my mother were all part of it. Exactly how my mother fitted into those earlier years I am not at all clear. My father was particularly remote during this time.

Early on, I slept in the night nursery with John, and then, when Elizabeth arrived, with her, and of course Nanny slept with us. When I was seven, my sister Bridget was born; so I had to move from the night nursery to a room on my own. I thought I was really getting grown up at this stage. I also started going downstairs to the dining room for all meals, including the formal dinner. The latter I found lengthy and particularly tedious, though I was fascinated by the brushing away of crumbs or other debris on the table by Kelly between courses.

I had dolls and a dolls' house out in the garden. My special doll was Sally, for whom my mother made a most wonderful wardrobe. Indoor pursuits included jigsaw puzzles and board games, principally Monopoly. Mah-jong, which we played with lovely hand-carved ivory pieces, became a favourite. John started stamp-collecting and bird-watching, and I became more involved in sewing.

I enjoyed roller-skating in the wintertime. The furniture was removed from the veranda, providing marvellous space and a terrazzo floor. I can vividly recall the exhilaration one wet Saturday, spending a couple of hours on my own just skating. I think it was the speed and, at times, the daring nature of this occupation that gave me an experience of elation, a real 'high'. I also associate the winter months with riding my pony in the fields and learning to jump, as well as going for riding lessons to Dudgeons, whose land along the Stillorgan Road is now part of UCD.

Racing around on our bikes and chasing each other was very much part of our lives in all weathers; 'our', in many instances, refers to John and myself. Although all of us siblings were born within a decade, there was just a year and two days between John and me. Elizabeth came three years after me, was the middle child and therefore liable to suffer from feelings of isolation, a common experience of children in this situation. It was only later in life I became aware that this indeed happened. Bridget was born four years later and then Monica just two years after her and they became great friends. I recall at Monica's birth that she came home with a nurse who stayed for a few days, a fact which happened for all of us following our births in the Leinster Nursing Home.

I loved climbing the great mulberry tree. I also enjoyed swinging on a rope between two other trees and if you were brave you could jump off onto either of the trees. In fact, whenever possible in winter, and always in summertime, whether during the holidays or after lessons, I loved being out of doors. I was always interested in what was going on – whether it was in the kitchen, with the hens or in the garden somewhere. In the summer months, I helped with the fruit-picking – raspberries, strawberries, gooseberries, redcurrants – until tennis took over a lot of my time.

From early on, I was brought to dancing classes: general dance, tap-dancing and later ballroom dancing. I see in my baby book that I went to my first dancing lesson to Miss Corry-Neale in September 1936 when I was only two. What I do remember about Miss Corry-Neale is, sadly, her funeral. I was still very young and it was my first meeting with death. I can recall going to the graveyard in the grounds of the Church of Ireland church in Enniskerry. We also went swimming and, in the summer months, could easily have gone two or three days a week by tram to Seapoint. I learned to swim when I was four. An incident there I well recall was from when I was trying to teach my brother to swim. He panicked, which resulted in his putting his hand on my head and keeping me under for what seemed like an age. Eventually someone spotted what was happening and came to the rescue. I also loved diving off the board into the sea. Miss Brennan gave me piano lessons and later I had tennis coaching with a Mr Paterson in Anglesea Lawn Tennis Club.

A key event, and one I remember every anniversary up to the present day (8 September), was my First Communion. I was prepared for it, as was my brother a year earlier, by a Marie Reparatrix sister in their convent on Merrion Square. The day itself began with getting into the white dress, then the Mass, where I knelt on a white prie-dieu up in front with the sisters and my family at the back. I had been told earlier that I could choose what I wanted to do that day. My choice was bicycle-chasing and Alan O'Grady showing me how to plant potatoes in a patch given to me inside the walled garden. So off with the dress but it later went on again when we returned to the convent chapel for benediction at 4 p.m. I knew something wonderful had happened to me that day; that God had come close, was not only around me but within me and filled me with a happiness too deep for words. In those days there were fewer distractions, with no party and no money or gifts of any kind. The emphasis was solely on the wonder of the event itself. I was gifted with and am intensely grateful that the Mystery of Faith, an alternative name for the Eucharist, became a profound reality in my life from then on. I was also gifted on that day with the awareness of how special I and everyone else is in God's eyes, and feel sad that so many are not blest with this realisation, or come to it only late in life.

My Confirmation had less of an impact. I had not yet gone to school, so I went on my own, wearing a blue linen dress, surrounded by schoolchildren in their uniforms. It took place in Blackrock Church in 1944, hence I would be just ten. Two things stand out: The bishop's question to me was, 'How many apostles were there?' to which I replied thirteen, since I included Judas' replacement. The bishop kept to the traditional twelve. The other was my mother's request that I should not stand up when the pledge about not taking alcohol was being made. She felt I was too young to take such a pledge.

The following year, in 1945, I started at Loreto Convent, Foxrock. I went there and back on the 63 bus, which stopped on Anglesea Road. I suppose I had been prepared for it, knowing that my educational path was to spend a year there and then go to boarding school. My mother felt I needed to acclimatise myself to other schoolchildren. She also insisted with the sisters that I would not go to Irish classes since I had, until then, learned no Irish and would not need it in my next school. I cannot remember getting involved in games but I presume I did. I made some friends, especially Helen. We visited each other's homes, but sadly, I suppose because a year was too short, none of these friendships lasted.

3

Life in Simmonscourt

Entertaining was an important part of life at Simmonscourt, and my parents had many formal dinner parties. Sometimes the guests were friends, other times, I think, probably business associates, occasionally some from the diplomatic corps, and often we did not know the guests. On really important occasions, the silver epergne was used as the centrepiece on the dining-room table, such as the time we hosted the world primate of the Benedictine Order. The table was always set with great care and enlarged if the numbers required it. On these occasions a cloth was never used. Sometimes we, the children, were introduced to the guests before they went to dinner and then we retired from the scene, but not necessarily to bed. I was fascinated when the meal was over and the women retired to the drawing room having 'powdered' themselves, while the men stayed on for their cigars and liqueurs and male conversation.

We had many children's parties: birthday parties, Christmas parties, tennis parties and so on. Our mother was great at indoor parties, since she had a vast repertoire of party games. My favourite was Crazy Post. The house was ideal for it. Boxes with place names on them were partially hidden around certain rooms in the house. Some central figure gave out the post name, you then had to run around looking for that box and then go back to get another name, until finally all the post was delivered and the first to do so was the winner. A quieter game usually followed, such as the tray game. A number of items (around twenty-five) were placed on a tray. You looked at them for a few moments, then the tray was taken away and you had to write down what you remembered. Another writing activity was when you were given a sheet of paper with a word containing a lot of letters and you had to make as many words as you could out of it. The classic word chosen was 'antidisestablishmentarianism'. Occasionally outside help was called on; I remember once we had a conjurer performing. Parties revolved around the billiard and dining rooms, never the drawing room.

The summer parties were another matter. All sorts of sports were arranged: high jump, long-jump races, relay races, obstacle races, three-legged races, tug of war, scavenger hunts, etc., as well as clock golf, croquet, quoits and tennis tournaments. John and I shared birthday parties as there was only a year and two days between us. We did, however, have two separate cakes – his was always chocolate and mine was always strawberry. A special party was always held on the Friday of Horse Show week at the RDS, when a lunch was laid on for those going to the Aga Khan Cup. Since it was a Friday, it was always salmon – a rarity in those days – followed by several desserts. The one thing I remember was the very large number of people who came each year. The RDS always remained a dominant presence in our lives, from the backdrop sound of the clock chiming at regular intervals, to always attending the annual Spring and Horse Shows and other events like the Dog Show on St Patrick's Day.

Overnight visitors were largely family. My mother's three brothers all stayed from time to time. The most regular was Uncle Henry, who came every year. He was a warm, lively person who always added spark to the place. He occasionally brought a priest friend on his visits, as did my half-brother, Jim. A couple of my mother's English friends also stayed, including Jane Stewart, who, I think, introduced our parents to each other. There were others, but memory fails. Regular day visitors were Uncle Jim, who cycled down from Milltown Park most Sundays to join us for lunch.[22] Lunch and dinner were always announced by the ringing of a great gong. Aunt Louis was another regular visitor, who when her husband, our Uncle Arthur, died, came to live in Dublin. In the last year of my father's life, W.T. Cosgrave visited regularly. He came across to me in my brief encounters with him as a humble, kind and gentle person with a beautiful smile. I think he knew better than any of us my father's state of health when he was close to death. I had no idea he was such an important figure in Irish life at the time, and shows how poorly informed I was about Irish history and politics.[23] Peggy, our half-sister, and her three children, Antony, Robin and Susan (who were younger than John and me but Susan fitted between Bridget and Monica), also visited frequently. Tommy Bodkin was a colourful and popular presence, as well as a great talker, who was interested in many things and was well known in the art world.[24] Other regulars included the McMahon and Scroop families. Dr Scroop was the doctor at the mental hospital in Dundrum, where he lived in the grounds with his family, and we used to go to the occasional parties behind those high walls. We often had friends to visit, especially on Saturdays or Sundays. This started after John went to school and brought his

---

[22] Jim entered the Jesuits when he was 24, having previously worked as a stockbroker in his father's office. An interesting note in the *Irish Province News* (April 1951) says 'In the nineties of the last century the McCanns, father and son, who were probably the most successful stockbrokers of their day in Ireland, did warn their country against the triumphant credit system then in vogue, and universally deemed "as safe as the Bank of England" – the most popular comparison on the lips of men till 1914.' As a Jesuit he taught in Belvedere, was bursar in Clongowes and Gardiner St, and director of retreats in Milltown Park. In 1917 he became a military chaplain in the Great War, despite poor health. He remained until the end and went to Germany with the occupying troops. I remember we had a picture in the dining room which contained the medals he won during the war. I also recall he was a heavy smoker.

[23] Recently I spoke to Liam Cosgrave, W.T. Cosgrave's son, who is now in his nineties. He said he remembered my father 'Jack' well, used to visit Simmonscourt at times with his father and knew my half-brothers and sisters by name. He also recalled my father visiting their home regularly – facts I was completely unaware of. According to Liam, their friendship began by their both being members of the Ward Union Hunt. All these factors indicated the strength of their friendship, a fact which I had only previously surmised.

[24] Thomas Bodkin was director of the National Gallery from 1927 to 1935.

new school friends around. I have vivid memories of joining with them in two great pursuits: in winter, it was 'Fairy's Den', a great game of chase that covered the entire grounds; and in summer it was, of course, tennis.

We were a keen picnicking family. For our parents' birthdays, both at the end of August, we, for several years, took a picnic to the waterfall at Enniskerry. Another spot, and a whole day's outing, were trips to Ireland's Eye. I loved going out in the rowing boat, then climbing to the top through all the bracken and inevitably being stung by nettles. Those days nearly always seemed to be sunny. Another outing was to Stamullen, where my mother had a great friend, Sr Imelda, a Holy Child sister. We made further expeditions to our father's farm in Ratoath, where we would have lunch with his farm manager, Michael McCabe. A particular outing, which must have been during the war, was going to Easter Monday's race meeting at Fairyhouse in a horse-drawn coach. By request, I was allowed to sit in front with the driver. We occasionally went to watch our father or half-brother Paddy playing polo in Phoenix Park on a summer Saturday afternoon. On the odd Sunday, we would go for the day to Brittas Bay.

My parents spent their honeymoon in San Sebastian, and visited the Canary Islands after the war. Apart from one further trip my father took to India for a polo holiday with some friends, I do not remember them going abroad. Their haunt was an annual two weeks to the hotel in Parknasilla, Co. Kerry, in September or October. All of us children were convinced that we were conceived in that place because all our birthdays occur during the Gemini period. When I think of Parknasilla, I also think of letters. My first letters were posted to the hotel and the first postcards we received also came from our parents in Kerry. We never accompanied them, with Nanny being firmly in charge while they were away. I do remember, from the age of about ten, my mother giving me the keys of the storeroom, which I duly went to daily to give out to the cook whatever she needed. Early training in what responsibility entails.

I know from early photographs that John's and my first holidays were in Trearddur Bay on the island of Anglesea. I think we went a couple of times before the war broke out. My mother, Nanny, the pair of us, and some other friends of the family made up the party. I have a faint memory of staying in the Grand Hotel in Malahide. More clearly, I recall happy holidays in the Claremont Hotel in Howth and, another summer, we rented a house in Sutton. I enjoyed enormously spending hours making sandcastles – elaborate affairs with shells and greenery added as part of the landscape. Although Nanny came with us, I think our mother only came to visit. We also had a holiday in Donabate, to which we went by pony and trap. As we got older, and the war ended, we spent several summers in succession in Brittas Bay, renting a house for a month.

Christmas was always a big event. The ritual started in November, when we helped with the stirring of the mixture for the puddings. (There were two mixes, one with no alcohol for the Poor Clare nuns.) Festivities began on Christmas Eve, helping to decorate the tree in the billiard room. This room then became out of bounds for the rest of the day. Before bedtime, the crib was set up on the landing. In later years, we went to midnight Mass, although when we were very young it was on Christmas morning. Soon after breakfast, we were allowed back into the billiard room, where each of us had a special chair on which our presents were laid out. It was a time when I always remember feeling thoroughly spoiled. My mother delighted in giving presents and always loved Christmas. I also have a keen memory of the first year John and I had the idea of buying our parents a gift. After much serious thought, we decided on buying a red cyclamen plant, which we duly purchased in Drummonds of Dawson Street.

At 11 a.m. sharp, my parents and the five of us and Kelly would go to the kitchen, collect the soup, dinner and desserts and, of course, the pudding, and processed with these through the shrubbery to present them to the Poor Clare sisters. On our return, I would help my mother set the table in the servants' hall in Christmas fashion, as they had their main dinner at midday. Precisely at 4 p.m., the doorbell would ring to announce Santa's arrival. More excitement! Then, not long after, the Barry family – Dermot, Brian and their mother – would arrive for dinner

(Dermot having played the part of Santa – we never made the connection, or never wanted to.) Dinner was festive and my mother started a custom still practised today by two of my sisters. A 'pie' was the centrepiece of the table – the pie being a round cardboard container covered with white paper, which had inside it a present for each person at the table. At the end of the meal, we pulled on a red ribbon attached to each person's gift. The meal usually concluded with Chinese whispers and sometimes the matchbox game. The latter meant attaching the cover of a matchbox to your nose and then passing it around from one person to the other beside them. After dinner, the night ended with charades.

As a family, we were blest with good health. There was one scare when my youngest sister Monica was thought to have polio. Fortunately, that was not the case. I know, and can vaguely recall, that John and I had our tonsils and adenoids out, as was customary at the time. I remember receiving a Snow White doll and John got a puzzle to keep us amused while still in hospital. I had jaundice when I was about eleven and could only eat toast and golden syrup for days. Whether it was because we only had minor illnesses, none of us ever went to bed in the daytime. It was simply a thing that was never done in the household. However, I do remember developing a bout of asthma during our summer holiday in Sutton. I had to be brought home, much to my dismay, and actually slept in my parents' room. It was the only time I recall that happening for any of us.

Our GP was Dr Frank O'Grady, but we rarely seemed to need him to call to the house or to visit him in his surgery. When I was seventeen, I clearly remember driving to Killiney to collect my two youngest sisters from school. On the way back, I developed acute abdominal pain. By the time we arrived at Simmonscourt, I had to be lifted out of the car and within two hours I was in St Vincent's Hospital. I was whisked off for surgery to have my appendix removed by 'Pops' Moran. My concern after the operation was not my health, but which of my (male) friends would come to visit me, particularly those who had started at medical school and who I knew were working in St Vincent's. Our dentist, Mr Stewart, was a jovial person and I did not mind my visits to him too much. For several years I had to wear bands (now called braces) on my teeth and was referred to a Mr Friel, who came across as a strange character – orthodontics was still in its infancy at the time.

***

You could say we were born into a rather religious household, with a nun and a priest on my father's side of the family and a priest on my mother's side. Our faith was rarely spoken about, but it was a backdrop that permeated our lives – similar to many households at the time, I imagine. Having the Poor Clares beside us and an oratory in the house, and religious relatives, presumably made the presence of a living faith somewhat more pronounced. When Uncle Henry and half-brother Jim came to visit (sometimes bringing their priest friends), they said their Mass each morning at the Poor Clares. Having them among us made religious life seem normal. There was no question of any of them being on pedestals or us putting them there.

The oratory was at the top of the house near Gaga's room. It was frequented, even if for no other reason, because it contained the hot press, and was furnished with an altar and three large statues of the Sacred Heart, Mary and St Joseph. It had proper benches, two small rows of them, and a set of stations. My father used to say a rosary there during Lent, in which some of the servants would join him. There was a sanctuary lamp, which I came to love, especially in my later teens – coming back home late at night from dances, seeing the warm welcoming red glow of it as we drove up the lane. Apart from the oratory and the large crucifix our parents had on their bedroom wall, there were no great symbols of religion around the house. When I was quite young, I had a devotion to St Therese, the Little Flower, as she was commonly known. In fact, the first book I think I ever read was the story of St Therese written for children – I even made a little altar in her honour.

As children we always went to Sunday morning Mass at the Poor Clares. A bench was set aside for the McCann family on the right side. Our parents usually went to Sunday Mass at the Sacred Heart Church in Donnybrook, our parish church, and where all of us were baptised. We went there every alternate Saturday morning for confession, again the custom of the time. I recall often going in jodhpurs on my way back from riding lessons.

I may not be objective enough to describe what the family culture was like. In a sense it was Anglo-Irish despite my father being Irish through and through. Possibly his father being an MP and he and his other two brothers having gone to school in England may have accentuated this Anglo-Irish element. My mother's background could highlight it further, plus the three oldest of us going to boarding schools in England. As a consequence, our accent was not pure Dublin but had a slight English intonation to it.

It did not happen often but one thing I remember my father liked was to sit at the piano and play by ear while singing Percy French songs and other Irish ballads. We had a large radio set in a cabinet and a His Master's Voice gramophone, which played 78 records. When long-playing records came in, we got a new machine. It was around then that John became interested in classical music (later for him to become a passion, especially opera) and through him I also started to appreciate classical music in general. The first LP I received that Christmas was of *Die Fledermaus*, which I played and replayed the entire holidays. Our father had some connection with the Theatre Royal, so we sometimes went there for performances. What they were I cannot recall, but I remember the dancing and especially the Royalettes. On one occasion at the Royal, I had to present the President, Seán T. O'Kelly, and his wife with a bouquet. We went every year to pantomimes, but I rarely remember going to more serious theatre.

A copy of the *Irish Times* and *Irish Independent* were left out each morning at breakfast, which I only glanced at for certain items, like the tennis results. In hindsight, the biggest lacuna for me was not the lack of books but a diminished prominence given to the value of reading. John was an exception and read a great deal, starting with the *Just William* series and then the Henty books, followed by a widening interest in all manner of books. I started off with Enid Blyton, and began *Little Women*, but it did not grab me. I really only began reading seriously in my late twenties, when I was introduced to theology. This was partly due to being drawn to the outdoors as well as being involved in more active pursuits.

Our important neighbours were, of course, the Poor Clare nuns in St Damien's Convent. May, my grandparents' eldest and only girl, was a delicate child. She was a very small baby and it was thought she would not survive. The story goes that, when travelling in the Carlow area as a young woman, May heard a bell ringing and discovered it was coming from a Poor Clare convent. She immediately felt drawn to enter, did her novitiate in a monastery in Manchester in 1898 and returned to Carlow in 1899, where she was professed and took the name of Sr Mary Magdalen. This seemed a quick progression – was it due to ill health I wonder? The number of women joining Carlow grew beyond the capacity of the place, so May approached her parents asking if St Mary's Lodge, a house in the grounds of the then Simmonscourt demesne, could be given over to establishing a new convent.[25] She had been told as a child that a church originally stood on the grounds of Simmonscourt and her desire was to bring back the Blessed Sacrament to that place. Her parents willingly agreed. At first, her father approached the archbishop but failed to get permission. However when May's mother tried, it seems Archbishop Walsh was unable to refuse his friend and verbally gave the go-ahead for the new foundation.

As babies, we were all presented to the nuns. We were handed to the sisters through a roundabout turn and they would pick us up on the other side inside the enclosure. When outside

---

[25] When my grandparents bought Simmonscourt Castle, it included St Mary's Lodge. This lodge was rented to the Lynch family who, in the words of Fr Crean, 'kindly vacated it' to allow the sisters' takeover. A new convent was built in front of this house, the house itself being incorporated into part of the convent. This work was completed in 1912. Sr Magdalen and my grandmother are buried in the convent graveyard. It was only about twenty years ago when, as a community physiotherapist, I was allowed into the enclosure to treat one of the nuns and saw these graves for the first time.

the grille, you can only touch the sisters with your fingers. It remains the same to this day. Over the years, we visited from time to time and always at Christmas but, of course, we could see the nuns at Mass in the distance, again through a grille. The convent left its imprint on all of us in varying ways.

4

From Boarding School to My Father's Death

In September 1946, when I was twelve, I was sent to boarding school. John had gone to the Benedictine boarding school
at Downside, in Somerset, a year earlier. Now it was my turn
to go to the Holy Child School at Mayfield in Sussex. In the
early years, travel was by the mail boat to Holyhead and the
train to Euston, where Uncle Bernard would meet me and
bring me across London to Victoria Station and put me on the
train to Mayfield. This, and the return route, took place three
times every year. It was just one year after the war and there
were still newsreel cinemas in all the stations, to which I recall
going, especially in Victoria. The travel was not all on my own,
as usually a band of about seven other Irish girls going to the
same school largely stayed together. I used to love that moment
coming home for holidays, when we got into Dublin Bay and
you could see Dun Laoghaire emerging into view in the early
morning light. In the last year of school we flew, from Dublin
airport to Norfolk airport.

On my second journey home, for the Easter holidays, on the
train from Euston to Holyhead, I realised, when called in my
sleeper by the porter at 3 a.m., I had lost my boat ticket. Tears
were plentiful. With the others around me, I was allowed on
the boat. It was at this moment I became aware that I was older
now, twelve years old, and must take responsibility for my own

life; in other words, in that instant I grew up. I think, in hindsight, that one of the values of boarding school is this realisation that we have to learn to make decisions about things and not be overly dependent on our parents and others.

I was happy at school. I loved the spacious and beautiful grounds, the school itself and particularly the chapel, which was renowned for its beauty and for having the widest Gothic arch in the country. When I started off I was academically on a similar level as others in my class but as the years progressed I slipped somewhat. One reason was that I was probably not as bright as several of the other girls. A further reason was that I became very involved in sport. I loved gym classes and continued with dancing lessons, but mainly I became good at hockey and ended up being captain of the First Eleven. I was also captain of the First Six tennis team, and played netball – all of this despite having the nickname 'Fatty' at school. I did not experience the latter as bullying. Maybe the realist in me knew it to be true and the fact I was good at games must have compensated. I was the second head of the school in my last year and this must also have helped me overcome possible feelings of being ostracised because of my size.

The teachers were great people and Mrs Vesey was my favourite. She taught geography and biology and as a result these became my favourite subjects. There were three outstanding sister teachers whom we knew to be highly competent in their field: Mother Elizabeth (English), Mother Ignatius (art) and Mother Consiglio (music). Even then I appreciated the ethos that the Holy Child sisters gave us. For instance, I remember how they inculcated in us the understanding that when you were left on your own in a situation, whether as a class or an individual, you acted with even greater responsibility and care than if someone was there to overlook your behaviour. Mother Declan (Matthews), an Irish woman, was headmistress. I, like most of the girls, admired and respected her. She also acted as a career guidance teacher and so in our last year at school we were invited in to talk with her about our possible futures.

During those school years, three separate incidents come to mind. The first concerned my inability to learn things by heart.

This seemed essential in English class with poetry, Shakespeare and so on, and I just could not and never have been able to do it. As a result, I fared poorly in English from then on. I think this inability got in the way of my appreciating literature of all kinds. I am sure this is the reason why to this day I shy away from reading poetry, always pre-judging my inability to understand it. It also had something to do with my confidence concerning speaking in public. I remember the agony in my last year when we all had to talk about a topic for five minutes in front of the class and I just could not do it. An Irish girl in the class suggested I talk about the Dublin Horse Show, which should have been easy; I simply freaked out. The second incident, a conscience dilemma, came about as follows. I had been invited to John's final prize-giving day in Downside. My parents were over for it and I had permission to go. I was to get to Bath by train. As it turned out, I was playing in a rather vital tennis match against another school. My game went to the third set, which meant I might not catch my train. The dilemma: should I fight on or just quickly lose the set? I decided the better thing to do was to be loyal to the team. Hence I fought on – a long set. I missed the train and also lost the match! I was asked recently in relation to this event, were my parents and John disappointed? I must admit I never thought about that and the answer is I do not know. I would like to think that my parents were proud of the decision I took.

The third was a very sad event. My half-sister Peggy sent her second son, Robin, to the Benedictine preparatory school at Worth, her brother Jim being at this time a monk at Downside Abbey. Tragically, Robin, who was around twelve at the time, sleepwalked out of a window two storeys up and died instantly. Worth was relatively close to Mayfield and so I was able to go to his funeral Mass, where, naturally, both his parents were distraught. All I remember of Robin was that he was a quiet child and had beautiful fair hair. Antony, Robin's brother, was in senior school at Downside and he stayed there waiting for the hearse to arrive for Robin's burial in the monks' graveyard. I am not sure if Susan (Robin's sister) was at his funeral. My siblings and I have over the years grown very fond of Susan in our own individual ways and she has always been hospitable towards us.

I did my School Certificate with reasonable ease but did not go forward for the Higher Certificate. I certainly did not feel I could reach those academic heights and perhaps the teachers thought likewise. It also meant staying on a further year. Since there were no plans or ambition on the part of my parents that I go to university (unlike John, who was always considered the brainy one, as indeed he was), they expressed no inclination for me to stay on at school and so I left shortly after my seventeenth birthday.

I was sad to leave, partly because I loved everything about the school and also because I was very unclear about the future. Thoughts of a vocation had been discussed with Mother Declan but I was uncertain about the idea. I do know that my religious faith deepened considerably during my school years. Nothing was forced on us. For instance I found myself wanting to get up early and go more frequently to daily Mass of my own accord.[26] I loved the yearly 'Forty Hours' (i.e. when the Blessed Sacrament is exposed for forty hours), when those who wished got up during the night to pray in the chapel for an hour. We also had good priests, mostly Jesuits, giving annual retreats, which were times of special fervour, as was the day I was enrolled as a Child of Mary. I remember preparing for it with great intensity and then the joy of the day itself.

My mother intuitively understood my inner struggle on leaving school and came over for the final prize-giving day and the next day took me to Glyndebourne for a treat. I cannot even remember what opera was on. The place is so enchanting, especially on a sunny evening, with dinner at the interval out of doors and everyone wearing evening dress. I see my time at Mayfield as being a very rich experience. I was, and am, grateful for the opportunities it offered, included the making of good friends.

---

[26] This practice of going more frequently to daily Mass continued in the holidays. At Easter time, I also became involved in helping Miss O'Sullivan, the sacristan to the Poor Clares, especially in Holy Week. In pre-Vatican II days, the ceremonies were very elaborate and lengthy.

Being back in Simmonscourt during school holidays meant for me, above all, being reunited with John. When we were small, we played together all the time. We had our fights: for example, he once hit me on the head with a croquet mallet when I beat him for the first time. As the years went on, and especially during these holiday periods, we grew very close – truly fond of each other. I recall one day walking down Anglesea Road with him, hand in hand, feeling very happy and thinking no one could have a brother so close as he was to me and me to him. Thankfully that relationship remained and grew until he got married, when, as in all inter-sibling relationships, a marriage partner changes many things.

During the holiday periods, life at Simmonscourt continued much the same as before. In summer, the focus was on tennis: tennis practice, tennis parties and tennis tournaments at Fitzwilliam and Lansdowne Lawn Tennis clubs. John and I always played in the mixed doubles for these tournaments. John was really good and I was not bad. When things got tense in a match, I can still hear him say to me 'just get it back' – in other words just get the ball over the net even if you can't play a good shot. I remember also liking to sunbathe and would lie for lengthy periods outside the dining-room folding doors. I think it was a time when I touched something that today I would call contemplation. I had a real sense that God was close and in the environment all around me. In the Christmas holidays, we went to ballroom dancing classes together. John became a good dancer and I always enjoyed dancing with him. I went on to get certificates in ballroom dancing, firstly my bronze medal and then silver, but failed in the gold. It was a great disappointment but at the same time I sense this was a key moment that helped me to see how you have to get over disappointments and move on. As we became older, dance parties in each other's friends' homes became more common. I loved dressing up for these. Annie, the seamstress, was called on to make evening dresses for these occasions and I can still visualise many of them. I loved the dancing most of all, but remember too those awful moments of 'would I be asked up to dance?'

In the Easter holidays of 1950, a Holy Year in Vatican terms, I joined the Downside pilgrimage to Rome. John was there, of course. It was wonderful seeing all the sites of this great city and to visit all four basilicas. Amidst the fervour and excitement on Good Friday, we were sitting in a café on the Via della Conciliazione tucking happily into bacon and eggs. Only at the end did I realise we had broken both the fasting and abstinence laws, and on one of the holiest days of the year. All we could do was laugh at what we had done and the incongruity of the situation.

The summer after leaving school, I had my 'coming-out' dance. It was a grand affair and, as it turned out, it was the last big party to be held in Simmonscourt. Both drawing rooms were cleared and popular Peggy Dell and her ensemble provided the music. My mother had part of the garden floodlit. There were many guests, including school friends from England who came and stayed in the house. You were sure to be invited to dance as all the male guests were expected to try to have one dance with the hostess. I thoroughly enjoyed the evening but the more significant happening occurred later. Around 3 a.m., the family and guests all drifted off to bed. I stayed up in the study listening to records. I could not go to bed because I just had an intense longing to go to early morning Mass at the Poor Clares. I knew then that that was more important to me than all that went on before, enjoyable though it had been. In other words, it was pointing to the fact that my heart lay in another place.

That autumn it was decided that instead of going to finishing school for three months, which many girls did, I would go and live with a family in Paris and learn the language. However, the experience proved to be a disappointment. The family took me nowhere and rarely spoke to me at table, which meant that my French did not progress. That may not entirely be their fault, as I discovered later, when trying to learn Italian, that I have no ear for languages. Fortunately, Uncle Leon lived in Paris, so he took me out occasionally. Also my half-brother Paddy came over and took me to the Longchamp races and after that to a nightclub, my first. This was a bitter-sweet experience, as Paddy himself suddenly took a drink after a period of abstinence. I was aware in a hazy way that Paddy had difficulties with alcohol but had never previously witnessed him drunk. In my late teens I had feelings of fear, shame and even sadness at people becoming drunk; whether my feelings were excessive or not, I am not sure. This led me to avoiding alcoholic drinks until I was about thirty. Now I enjoy a glass of wine with my meal as well as a gin and tonic.

Apart from these outings, I was left largely to my own devices, so I decided to get to know Paris. Every day I was out and about with guide book in hand seeing places, visiting all the great museums and art galleries, and even going to the opera on my own. Uncle Leon got tickets for a grand ball in honour of Princess Margaret and provided a chaperone. I did discover a convent near the apartment where I was staying that had perpetual adoration. I often went there for a visit and received great consolation in a way I could not describe; it was simply good to be there in that wonderful presence.

I came home in time for Christmas and John also returned after his term in Oxford, where he was studying Classics. After the Christmas ritual, John went back to university and my sisters to their schools, but what was I to do? I decided with my mother that I would finish the academic year out by enrolling in a domestic science course at Ballsbridge Technical College, which I enjoyed. However, the uncertainty of how I wanted my life to go forward was all the time pressing in on me. As it turned out, that particular year, after leaving school, and the two that were to follow proved to be the most stress-filled years of my life. It would seem that my time of crisis came at the end of my teens rather than at their beginning or middle period.

On a positive note, following my seventeenth birthday, three things happened. Firstly, I got my driving licence. No one really taught me. I watched carefully how people drove, how to use the gear box in particular and then got Kinch, the chauffer, to sit in with me as I took off gingerly and manoeuvred the car up and down the front drive. It felt fantastic. Then my mother felt I should be given an annual allowance in order to teach me how to manage money responsibly. As a result, a bank account was opened and I had my own cheque book. This money was primarily for buying clothes and other small goods that I might need. The allowance was £100 per year – a lot of money for a seventeen-year-old girl in those days. I discovered that in today's values it would be €2,300. The third and perhaps most important event came out of doing some voluntary work. My mother's friend Carmella O'Grady asked me if I would help out in the Infant Aid Society. This charity gave out free milk to poorer children under the age of two. What it meant in practice was that every month I visited families to deliver vouchers for this scheme. The area I was allocated was in some of the tenements off Gardiner Street. The families were lovely but I was shocked at the poverty. This abruptly awakened in me a keener social consciousness – something I am grateful for, even if my involvement never reached the intensity of Alice Leahy or Peter McVerry sj.

I decided I would train for nursing. Since my half-sister Mary trained at the Middlesex Hospital in London, I decided to apply there. Around May I went over for an interview and narrowly scraped in to do the course. Two reasons for not passing then emerged: my blood pressure was low and I was too small. I should have been an inch taller! In the end I was accepted to start the following September. I also recall that year spending a weekend with John in Oxford. I was amazed by Oxford and all the quaint college buildings spread throughout the town. John lived within his college, Exeter, and so I was unable to stay there. He got me a B&B right in the centre of the town. It was exciting to get a glimpse of what college life was like and meeting his friends. A memory that remains is of people all over the place wearing black gowns and with bundles of books under their arms as they strode about, presumably going from one college to another.

During the winter of that year, my father had a second, severe hunting accident. No bones were broken but it left him unwell and, looking back, I can see now that he never recovered from that incident. Coming into summertime, he became increasingly frail and I recall, about six weeks before he died, that I would sometimes take him out for a drive in the afternoons. Indeed, I did so the day before he died. We, however, had no idea that he was so close to death. I recall that night of 24 August 1952 so clearly because it was his birthday. John and I were out at a big dance at the Maguires, a family we knew well over the years and frequently visited because they had a swimming pool, but also because they were very hospitable people. We came home at about 2 a.m. to find our half-brother Paddy standing and waiting for us at the back door as we drove up the lane. I thought he was drunk but instead he greeted us with the words 'Our father is dead.' I was astonished. We went in immediately to my mother. Apparently, around midnight he had got up to go to the toilet and dropped dead just beside my mother's bed. The doctor had already been when we arrived and said it was a heart attack. My mother came in to sleep in the bed beside me in my room and stayed there for a week.

My father was laid out at home for two days. There was no wake, just a few callers. The funeral Mass was in Donnybrook parish church. My mother, John, Elizabeth and myself attended the Mass and went home afterwards, except for John. It seemed that in those days women did not go to the cemetery after funerals. I never saw the grave until 35 years later, when my mother died. My father's death meant, in the immediate future, that John and I had to cancel a booking we had made to go that September to the Edinburgh Festival. I also decided it would not be right to go off to London a month later, feeling somehow that my mother needed me around.

In the days and weeks following his death, life became subdued. Although it was never mentioned, everyone knew that this was the end of life in Simmonscourt. My mother had the onerous task of finding us a new home and of dispersing the staff. Living in my own personal haze at the time, I remember very little about how all this took place. My memory is less acute about what happened then than it is about the earlier years. I recall nothing of the problems about letting staff go, arranging what went to whom, and where, etc. I was however interested in the buying of the new house and where it would be. The whole process of winding up Simmonscourt and the final sale – not to the RDS as many people thought, but to a group called Irish Estates – took over a year. They converted the house into apartments and built houses and apartment blocks in the grounds and later sold one of the fields to the RDS, now known as the Simmonscourt Extension.

***

In hindsight, we had been living a charmed existence. I appreciated, enjoyed and felt blest by it all. At the same time, like all teenagers, I did not want to be different. The phrase I so resented was the comment sometimes made by people, along the lines of, 'She is one of the McCanns from Simmonscourt, you know.' That comment implied that we were a family set apart. Of course there was some truth here in the sense that our physical situation was rather unique even among our friends, many of whom lived in quite big houses, yet none with the same size of grounds or number of servants. The experience must have coloured our lives. I hope and believe that none of us turned out to be snobs. My father was obviously a successful business and sportsman and lived a life very similar to that of his father. I do not think he thought of himself to be a cut above other people. My mother certainly never exuded vibes of grandeur or importance; if anything, the opposite was the case. Both parents were hospitable and enjoyed sharing Simmonscourt with others. I know that quality of life is not founded on externals but on satisfying interpersonal relationships which can develop in the most impoverished surroundings. However, it is a blessing to have pleasing surroundings while at the same time realising that, 'despite' or 'because of' whatever our background, loving relationships can flourish.

To this day, it truly amazes me that my grandfather was born before the Famine began. It was also interesting to learn about his life and then see how the lives of his children evolved – and finally how we, his grandchildren, benefitted in the way we did. It leaves me with a great sense of gratitude.

Part Two

RELIGIOUS LIFE

5

Discerning a Vocation

In early 1953, my mother began to look in earnest for a house for us all. I became interested in that search and I think we moved in the summer of 1953. The concentration was so much on the new home that leaving the old and the world that went with it did not impinge on my thoughts and feelings in the way, with hindsight, one might have thought it would. My mother wanted somewhere in the vicinity and we ended up not far away, on Merrion Road. There were two bedrooms for the four of us girls, one each for my mother and brother and a very small one for a maid; we had a maid for the first year, but then my mother felt she could manage on her own, especially as she became more competent and confident about the cooking end of things.

During the autumn and winter of 1952 into 1953, I attended a typing and shorthand course at Mrs Littleday's in South Frederick Street. I quickly mastered a good typing speed but took longer to become competent at shorthand. I was very pleased to have acquired touch-typing skills when computers appeared many decades later. I wonder today how many have that skill with their computers – do they learn it or work out their own system? Sometime in the spring or summer of 1953, Paddy, my half-brother, gave me a job at the family stockbroking office in Anglesea Street.[27] My hours were 10 a.m. to 4 p.m., Monday to Friday, and my weekly wage was £4.50. My office was small, dark and dingy, and the work very routine. I do not think I learned much and, certainly, very little about stockbroking. I did not have shares myself and neither have I ever owned any since. I do, however, recall writing many letters to solicitors.

I kept up my sporting activities. Tennis continued to take over in summer months, especially when John was home for holidays. In the summer of 1953, I entered Fitzwilliam and met 'Little Mo', Maureen Connolly, the then Wimbledon champion. I won one game and that largely on her mistakes. It meant that I qualified for the plate tournament (for those who were knocked out in the first round). I did reasonably well in this, so was seen around in my white dress up to the Friday before the finals. I played a bit of hockey with the Maids of the Mountains Hockey Club, having been introduced to this by my friend Daphne. I also dipped into two other sports: one was golf. Daphne and I played in Foxrock Club on Saturday mornings, but somehow it never appealed. The same with squash, where in those days it was difficult to find a court where women could play. Fitzwilliam was a possibility, but you had to go very early on a Saturday or Sunday morning, and if men appeared they were given precedence. For that reason, squash never really took hold; also being an indoor sport made it less appealing. What I enjoyed enormously was my weekly evening session at the League of Health. Kathleen O'Rourke, who founded this organisation in Ireland, suggested I come along. I am glad to know the organisation is still going strong today because it combined exercise and music.

Linking in with my sporting pursuits, I know I went on a skiing holiday sometime over the winter of 1952–1953. However I remain extremely vague about this event to the point of almost forgetting it happened, a significant factor in itself. It was a trip to Sestriere in the Italian Alps but I cannot remember what

---

[27] The premises backs onto what was the bank on Foster's Place. It is now the office of a solicitors' firm. They kept the original gate, which in the olden days enabled a carriage to be parked in that space.

group I went with and few other details. In a vague way I recall feelings of unease with myself and my place in society. In hindsight I sense my unconscious was at work indicating my life was being drawn in another direction. I can dimly recall the group going on a long bus ride to Milan to see Da Vinci's Last Supper but have no recollection of actually viewing the masterpiece. One clear positive remains, namely the great exhilaration I felt when on the last day I had mastered my skiing ability sufficiently to be able to let go on the slopes and so reach quite a high speed.

The dynamic at home became different in so many ways. Elizabeth stayed on at boarding school in England for two more years, John was still at Oxford, and Bridget and Monica went to school at the Holy Child Convent in Killiney, where they completed their secondary education. Christmas and the summer holidays led us to continue many of our previous activities – swimming, tennis, meeting friends and parties. John and his friend Dermot often went off on their bird-watching trips, particularly to the Bull Wall at Clontarf. I remember in particular the summer of 1953 when John brought his Indian friend Sushill, also a keen tennis player, to play at Fitzwilliam. John and I assumed he would stay with us, but our mother did not allow it, in case a bond developed between him and myself. Later in life I feel my mother would have made a different decision, as she grew more open to many things as each of us followed our own paths in life.

In hindsight, I see how difficulties concerning friendships inevitably arise when one goes to boarding school in another country. My friends at Mayfield became more distant simply from lack of contact, particularly so when soon my life took another direction. Parties still took place in each other's houses but only in holiday times. The family names I can recall included Collins, O'Grady, Maguire, Beatty, Miley, Hourihane, O'Connor, Lemass, Delamere, Carton, Carville, Quinlan, Martin, McGilligan, Byrne and Cruess-Callaghan. Daphne Dillon (née Collins) became my closest friend and we would have lengthy daily phone calls with each other. John became involved in small groups, where the focus was on listening to classical music, again in each other's houses. I did, periodically, spend quite a bit of time up in our attic listening alone to music. In particular, I recall and tingle when I think of listening to Maria Callas in Bellini's opera *I Puritani*. Another favourite of mine was Dietrich Fischer-Dieskau singing Lieder songs. Mozart, particularly his piano concertos and operas, was also on my special list.

Something of a romance began with a friend of John's called Crispin. In the spring of 1953, Crispin invited me to a May Ball at Cambridge, where he was studying. The most memorable part of the ball was its aftermath, when in the early hours of the morning, still in evening dress, we went punting down the river. The relationship continued at a distance and the following summer he came over and stayed with us in Merrion Road, but by then my life was moving in a new direction, leading to a crisis.

That direction was an inner call to do something more with my life and the best way seemed to be in religious life. I tried, at times, to shelve the idea but it kept coming back. This often happened at parties when, although I was enjoying myself, especially if dancing was involved, I was aware that something deeper in me suggested that my present way of living was not really for me. This led me to face two questions: firstly, did I have a religious vocation and secondly, which would be the right congregation for me to join? Regarding the second question, I knew I did not want to join a teaching order like the Holy Child Sisters, where I had attended school, or a contemplative order like the Poor Clares, nor did I feel drawn to a missionary order like the Medical Missionaries of Mary. Eventually I expressed my concern to a friend and he suggested I talk with Fr Crean, the Donnybrook parish priest. He had no hesitation in recommending the Irish Sisters of Charity.[28] This led to an appointment with Mother Teresa Anthony, the general of this congregation, the first of about four meetings with her taking

---

[28] Now known as the Religious Sisters of Charity. The name change became necessary as missions developed abroad, such as in Zambia, Nigeria, the United States and Venezuela, and with many houses in England.

place at their convent in Howth with its stunning views of Dublin Bay. The varied works of the congregation appealed and a particular attraction was that as well as taking the usual three vows of poverty, chastity and obedience, the sisters also took a fourth vow of service to the poor. This discerning process went on for over a year before I tentatively told Mother Teresa Anthony, in the spring of 1954, that I was seriously considering entering in October, the time for the next intake of postulants.

In autumn 1953, I had gone to Lourdes with my former nanny, her nephew and his wife. We set out in the nephew's Ford Prefect with myself as the second driver. We were to join the Dublin pilgrimage when we arrived but they did not make it because of a train strike in France. As a consequence, the previous set of pilgrims, a group of Germans, could not leave due to the same strike and the task then assigned to me was feeding the sick pilgrims in the hospital. I had never seen such disfigurement: several were war-wounded soldiers with horrific injuries. It was an eye-opener, but at the time it did not arouse in me any deep desire of wanting to formally care for the sick. I did have a sense of privilege in meeting these men and being able just briefly to help with their feeding.

Since it seemed likely in July of 1954 that I might be in the convent in October, I decided to 'do' Lough Derg – a three-day pilgrimage at St Patrick's Sanctuary – immediately followed by climbing Croagh Patrick on Reek Sunday. As I could not travel directly from Lough Derg in Donegal to Croagh Patrick in Mayo, this meant going by train to Dublin and then bus to Croagh Patrick. Some ardour! I have little memory of details. I think I merely had the satisfaction of having completed both, but not of receiving any great spiritual light. I do recall making use of the twenty-minute gap in Greenwich Mean Time between the east and west coast of Ireland to eat some food at twenty minutes to midnight. This meant keeping to the promise of fasting until midnight and yet allowing myself receive Communion on Croagh Patrick the next morning. One way of bending or working around rules.

Two events in the late summer of 1954 brought things to a head. Firstly, Crispin came to visit Ireland and stayed in our house. Things in the relationship moved up a few notches. To this day I cannot be certain whether I received a proposal of marriage but I think I did and my brother says I did. Then, later that summer, I went on a fantastic holiday with John, two of his Oxford friends and my half-nephew Antony. The focus of the visit was the Salzburg Festival and our method of transport was an old London taxi we called Matilda.[29] We bought her for £25 (only £5 each), picked her up in Liverpool and made two unscheduled stops on our way to Dover for repairs. This was a definite omen since, on arrival at Dover, the starter broke. From then on, this meant pushing Matilda to start, commencing with the arduous push up the ramp onto the ferry. From then on, we always tried to park on an incline. I was usually put in the driving seat while the other four did the pushing. John wrote about Matilda: 'Very soon she revealed her full range of faults: dodgy brakes, a leaking roof, the certainty that the engine would boil over on almost any incline, an inability to get started without being pushed, a complete absence of lights – but all these failings merely added to our enjoyment of the journey.'[30]

We finally arrived, having been a source of amusement and photograph opportunities for astonished Germans driving on the autobahns and overtaking Matilda at her stately 30 mph maximum speed. The plan was that after 'doing' the festival, two of the group, Bob and David, would go to Vienna for a few days, while John, Antony and myself would go to Venice. I recall an amusing incident on arrival. We went looking for a room for the three of us, explaining we were all related and one was my brother. The lady in charge of the *pensione* would not hear of it but when I asked if there was a church nearby and the time of Mass, she immediately relented. We had a wonderful time and then it was time to return to Salzburg, where we had left Matilda at a garage. We went only a short distance when more repairs were needed but within a few days, we were told

---

[29] A 1934 Beardmore.
[30] Sadly Antony, my half-nephew two years younger than me, died in his fifties and some years later his friends got together and published a book on his life. John wrote one of the contributions to this work, from which the above quotation is taken.

her condition was fatal. We made the rest of our journey by train and, because Matilda was a British-registered car, she could not be left to 'die' abroad so she was brought back to Dover where she was immediately scrapped. But what enjoyment she gave us all.

During the four or five days of waiting to bring Matilda back to Dover, I finally came to my decision to enter 'the Charities'. From all those years ago I can still vividly remember that small Bavarian village called Dettendorf, with its lovely little church where I was able to attend Mass and from where I wrote my letter to Mother Teresa Anthony saying I would like to join the October group. It was now September and I wanted an answer from her as soon as possible. So the deed was done and there was no turning back; I now knew that I was genuinely being called to religious life. On returning to England, John and I stayed with our Uncle Henry in Canterbury. It was there that I received a phone call from Mother Teresa Anthony saying my request had been accepted. Then I was back to Dublin with less than four weeks to go. My two youngest sisters did not believe me until I showed them some of the underwear we were supposed to bring with us.[31]

My main concern, as the time got closer to entering, was my mother because I was the first to properly leave home. My brother, of course, had left when, after boarding school and Oxford, he completed his national service and then got a job in England, where he has lived for most of his life. My mother made no complaints about me leaving home but I sensed it was difficult for her. The pain of parting, no matter what the reason, is normally an experience of grieving. The loss for the person who stays behind must be greater, since the one who leaves is often embarking on an adventure, which was true from my side of this equation.

---

[31] Absent on the list were bras. My mother was horrified and insisted that I bring some and wear them.

6

Formation Years

Monday 11 October 1954, 1 p.m., was the set date and time for my arrival at the Novitiate House at Mount St Anne's, Milltown, a journey from my home of about seven minutes by car. I decided it would be too stressful for my mother to bring me, as she would then have to drive home alone. Instead, I asked Alan O'Grady, now a medical student, if he would do the necessary and leave me at the convent door, and he duly obliged. I rang the bell as Alan drove away and was greeted by Mother Teresa Anthony and the novice mistress, Mother Mary Vincent, both of whom seemed surprised at finding me alone. After a brief few words of welcome in the parlour, I was introduced to a novice, who was called 'my angel'. She was to take special care of me for the first week, show me to ropes so to speak. And away I went with her into this new world. Twenty-three other newcomers arrived that same day. I was number five. It was the largest number of entrants the congregation had ever seen. The 1950s seems to have been the great decade for vocations in Ireland, especially of the apostolic religious type as opposed to the contemplative orders. The year 1954 had possibly the highest number due to it being the Marian Year (a year specially dedicated to Mary throughout the universal Church).

My angel brought me to my allocated room, or rather my cell. I was so glad we all had individual rooms, as I knew of other congregations who had to sleep in dormitories. The cell was utterly simple, which immediately appealed. The bed, covered with a blue and white check cover, a chair, a bedside locker and a press were the only pieces of furniture. The walls were bare except for a crucifix. I was introduced to the postulant outfit and asked to change. It was a black blouse and skirt with a bonnet, which had a short veil attached. This would be my garb for the next six months, the length of time normally allocated for postulancy. I presume I unpacked. We were asked to bring with us underwear, a dressing gown, black shoes and a watch. We had no other personal items. This did not bother me; in a sense I almost relished the simplicity of it all. I recall some friends saying to me, 'How did you leave behind all you were used to having?' I knew then, as I know even better now, that it is not possessions that bring happiness. Also, I knew that whether we give up many or only a few things is irrelevant. Relinquishing something very small yet precious might be more costly to a person than someone who relinquishes a great deal. In both cases, what matters is our attitude, whether it is one of possessiveness or non-attachment to whatever we own. Only the latter brings true freedom. However, the journey towards this goal takes a lifetime.

That evening we gathered in a small room and were given a pep talk by the assistant mistress of novices, Sr Emillian. She was, as I discovered over time, a silent, shy and rather self-effacing person. Over the years, I realised she was a very kind woman too. Her role was largely to look after our health needs, our clothing and other practical matters. We did not mix very much with the other novices for the first week, but continued with talks from varying sisters who introduced us to our new way of life. Throughout the week, I suppose we were sizing each other up as personalities began to emerge. Most were around seventeen, having come straight from school. Two were certainly in their thirties; one had been a nurse and the other a teacher. The amazing thing was that, even by the end of the novitiate, namely after two and a half years, we knew very little about each other. We did not talk about our families, our interests, and what we had done with our lives up to this point. That simply was the way it was and everyone just settled into that fact. You could say it was very impersonal and yet that was not right either. Obviously we warmed more towards some people than others and there was normally a sense of comaderie but in the background lay the rule which spoke of avoidance of 'particular friendships'. Our conversations I do not really remember but I think they were largely about the small happenings of everyday living.

That first week completed, we started in earnest to follow a certain daily routine, which became the pattern for the entire time we spent in the noviceship. The programme went largely as follows: wake-up call 5.30 a.m.; private meditation in chapel for one hour; Mass was at 7 a.m., followed by breakfast, after which we returned to 'make-up' our cells; then a period of manual work, where different tasks were allotted each week. These were largely all manual and mainly involved cleaning, as well as sorting laundry, setting tables and serving meals. There was half an hour given to spiritual reading, time for a walk in the grounds on one's own saying the rosary, and, in between, time for sewing. The first table dinner was at 3 p.m., followed by recreation. This time was spent sitting around the long noviceship table, chatting. There were communal prayers, called litanies, said before supper, which was at 7 p.m. This led into evening recreation, followed by night prayer at 9 p.m. and then to bed. I embarked on the programme easily enough and without much questioning. At the end of the first month, we received our first letters and first visit from family. With family visits you were allowed half an hour, with friends twenty minutes. I do not remember my first visit, but I recall my first letter, which was from John. It included a poignant quotation, which I think was from the playwright Christopher Fry: 'What if your freedom becomes my compulsion, what are we to make of this dilemma?' A pertinent question surely through all stages of life.

I had initially wondered how the convent fitted in such an influx of people when our 'set' arrived. Obviously, it had been achieved with some difficulty. A more long-term way of coping was to raise the roof and add a new storey, and this started soon after we arrived. A more immediate alternative was sending second-year novices to other houses. The extra squeeze due to the size of our group led to some of us postulants being sent out to other communities; this meant that after only five weeks, I was sent off to live in Howth, where there was a small community of seven. It was great. I became involved in what was going on and my main assignment was to go as 'companion on the mission' – the missioner being Sr Teresa Michael. This meant going out every morning from around 10 a.m. to 1 p.m. visiting people in their homes. Each call was unique; for example, some were to sick people, others grieving. In general, it was to people who had difficulties of some kind. As companion, my task was to simply listen. Some stories were more harrowing than others, but Sr Michael always seemed to be able to offer some comfort, either by her advice or by simply listening. Occasionally, she would pull some kind of goody out of her bag, which she always carried with her. This initiation was helpful to me later on.

The whole Howth experience was beneficial to me in many ways. I was living and praying with a wholesome group of women who were all involved in different tasks. I think, in some unconscious way, this window on what lay ahead once professed enabled me to cope with some of the oddities, and at time monotonous aspects, of novitiate life. I remember one incident, on 8 December 1954, when one of the worst storms of the century raged through Ireland. It was so dramatic seen from the advantageous position of the convent, and the lengthy period of lightening that lit up Dublin Bay was breathtakingly beautiful and truly awesome.[32]

---

[32] This convent in Howth was where I had my first interview with Mother Teresa Anthony. On that visit I noticed a plaque in the hall that referred to a John Judge O'Hagan and I sensed at that time there might be a family connection. In fact, there are three plaques. The first and largest says: 'Gleneveena [now known as Stella Maris] was given by the Honourable Mrs O'Hagan, now Sister Mary Francis, professed religious of the third order of St Francis, to the Irish Sisters of Charity, as a sacred memorial of her loved husband John Judge O'Hagan on condition that it should be maintained as a religious house and home of the ever Blessed Sacrament.' The second plaque says: 'Pray for the soul of John O'Hagan who died in this house, November 12th 1890'; and the third: 'Pray for the repose of the soul of Sr Mary Francis O'Hagan who died in Drumshambo 5th Nov. 1909.' Sr Brigid, recent Abbess at the Simmonscourt Poor Clares, says that the above Mary O'Hagan was a sister of my grandmother.

But my time in Howth ended unexpectedly. I was simply told I was to return to Mount St Anne's immediately. It was Christmas Eve. Of course I knew that my stay was not going to be forever, but to be recalled in such an abrupt manner and on the eve of Christmas I found hard to take. Returning was difficult enough, but when I awoke on Christmas morning, I became, for the first time, utterly homesick. I think it was the worst day of my novitiate. The intensity of the loneliness overshadowed me for the whole day. I was bodily living in Milltown but the rest of me was spent with my mother and siblings, who were all together. I relived with them every detail of their day, knowing it would be a repeat of the previous year, when my mother had resurrected the spirit of our 'Simmonscourt Christmas' in the new home in Merrion Road. John was home as usual and came to visit. Mother Teresa Anthony knew how important this would be for me and that our visits would be infrequent, and hence arranged that we could have a longer period of time together. I was grateful for that, yet at the same time was a bit uncomfortable – did it hint at a touch of favouritism? That was the last thing I wanted. I had about three of these visits with John over my noviceship period. The visits themselves always had a bittersweet hue about them.

Strangely, I can recall nothing about visits from my mother and sisters and the odd friend. There was an exception when one day, unexpectedly, I was called to the parlour. It was Peter Lemass, one of our friends and a keen tennis player. He was a year older than me but we shared the same birthday. At this stage, he was at Clonliffe studying for the priesthood. I was very touched by the fact he came to visit. Peter was later to live a particularly dedicated priestly life mainly in inner-city parishes and worked with the Radharc TV team. Another significant visit was from Mrs O'Grady (only years later could I call her Carmella), my mother's friend. She came to share with me a worry she had about a member of her family. I felt humbled that she came to me about it. It made me aware of the privilege, as well as responsibility, of being a religious. The experience enabled me to see that people trusted you with intimate matters and the sacred nature of that trust. Over those novitiate and early professed life years, I really lost contact with most of my friends, many of whom married during that time. There were two exceptions – Daphne Collins and Joan O'Grady – and, touchingly, both of them came to visit me on their wedding days.

Postulancy ended the day of our clothing in early May. In the first part of the ceremony, we entered in our bridal dresses. After the initial ritual was over, we came out and dressed in habits for the first time. Our hair was cut off so that the cap fitted close to the head and we wore a white veil. All 24 of us then processed back in and I think it was then we had Mass. We also received our new religious name. I chose Sr Paul Mary. I would have preferred Mary Paul, but there was already a sister with that name. Families were present at the ceremony and there was some form of celebration afterwards and, of course, photographs. I cannot recall any feelings around the day itself but I do know that inside myself was a wanting to enter my first novitiate year, called our 'spiritual year', as fully and as intensely as I could.

The full spiritual year canonically had to be lived within the novitiate itself. Regarding our weekly tasks, there were some 'jobs' people held for longer than a week. For example, the role of black-work mistress, who oversaw the making of habits, the white-work mistress, who looked after the making of caps and veils and altar linen, and the sacristan, who worked in St Gall's Church in Milltown village. Apart from taking my turn at some of the manual tasks previously described, I was for over six months assigned the job of manaductress, a kind of overseer of manual works who was also responsible for the general running of happenings in the novitiate. I loved the job and I think it, more than anything else, helped me to sail through that year. Others I know found life in the noviceship much more difficult. Having been to boarding school was also an added advantage, as for most of the others it was their first time away from home.

Meals were held in silence, with someone reading aloud from differing religious texts throughout. We sat at long tables, so the dishes were put at the top and then pushed along after each person had helped herself. I think we may have talked at supper, which was usually a simple meal of bread and jam. On

feast days, of course, we talked at all meals and had more elaborate food. Ingredients on the whole were good and nutritious,
with eggs and vegetables coming from the onsite farm. The farm
work and the cooking and other domestic tasks were done by
lay sisters. I was quite taken aback when I discovered there was
a two-tier system. As I understood it, women who wanted to
become sisters but did not have the educational opportunity of
going to secondary school entered under the term 'lay' despite
the fact that they took religious vows. It was during our noviceship that it was decided to change the title to 'second degree
sister'. I thought that was even worse. I am not sure whether it
was before or after the Second Vatican Council that that distinction was abolished, thank God.

It was our 'spiritual year': what nourished our spiritual
lives? In hindsight, very little, as I believe was the case in most
female religious congregations. I can see that this area was the
greatest weakness of our whole formation. We read the same
book on the spiritual life for thirty minutes daily, throughout
our whole noviceship. It was always referred to by everyone
simply as 'Rodriguez'. I cannot recall any of it. I think the book
was *Practice of Christian Perfection* by Alphonsus Rodriguez. We
had no input of any kind on scripture or theology. The novice
mistress did give weekly talks on the 'spiritual life'; these were
largely related to prayer and the vows. The majority of the latter
topic was focused on obedience, less on poverty and practically
nothing was said about chastity, which came up indirectly in
reference to the rules of 'custody of the eyes' and not developing 'particular friendships'. We had individual sessions with the
novice mistress from time to time. This was more about finding out how we were getting on and being told certain things.
It was not spiritual direction, of which we knew nothing. The
latter, in all fairness, has only developed in recent decades.

Every month, Fr James McMahon sj came and lectured us
on our rule book, which was almost word for word Ignatian-
based. The focus was always on the rules and never on the
Constitutions of the Religious Sisters of Charity; I do not know why
this was so. We knew from our reading of Mary Aikenhead's
life, our foundress, that she wanted the spirituality of the sisters

to be based on St Ignatius' spirituality.[33] The priests who said
Mass were nearly always Jesuits from Milltown Park and it was
Jesuits who gave the annual eight-day retreats and tridiums
(three-day mini-retreats held in Advent and Lent). I am very
grateful that one of the greatest heritages I received from our
formation and in later years was this Ignatian foundation to
my spirituality and the general outlook on life that this offered.
Even if this spirituality was poorly presented, its spirit was
always there, giving some kind of inner core to our living.

A communal prayer life punctuated the day. Our one-
hour early morning prayer was based on a set of meditations
set out for each day of the year. At 12 noon, we went to the
chapel together for our fifteen-minute midday examen, a kind
of examination of conscience/consciousness done in a prayerful way (again an Ignatian form of prayer). Late afternoon was
litanies, a communal exercise of vocal prayers that took the
place of reciting the Divine Office. (The Office was introduced
after Vatican II.) Then, at 9 p.m., we went for our last visit to
the chapel for night examen. This was followed by a short time
preparing for the next morning's meditation.

There was very little intellectual stimulation, with no newspapers, no library and no real opportunities for reading. This
must have been very painful for readers, but it did not bother
me. Neither was there any radio. Hence we were left unaware
of current events and other happenings, something I realised
later on when people would talk about films, songs, some fairly
major national and international events, and other matters of
which we knew nothing. Any free time we had, known as *ad
libitum*, usually found me sewing. I was already competent with

---

[33] Apart from Ignatius, a central focus in her life, as found in her many letters,
was the importance of divine providence in all the endeavours she undertook. For
example, her foundation in Foxford was known as Providence Mills. Also central
to her personal spirituality was the motto she chose for the Congregation: 'Caritas
Christi Urget Nos' ('The love of Christ urges us on'). I am indebted to her for both
these inspirations. While many external symbols of Christianity are disappear-
ing from both home and public life, it delights me when I see the Congregation's
motto shown in the Latin version on the uniform of St Vincent's Hospital staff as
well as on every paper napkin that patients use. In 2015, the Congregation cel-
ebrates the 200th anniversary of its foundation.

the needle and the sewing machine and came to enjoy making habits. There was little emphasis on exercise, apart from our daily walks saying the rosary. As a result of this I think I put on even more weight, eventually reaching eleven stone – and I am barely five feet in height.

As I look back on my life, it is strange how sport receded in a way I hardly noticed. On reflection, it illustrates the importance of context in human living. Practically all my sport was connected with Simmonscourt or boarding school, and of course John. While I dabbled a bit with golf, hockey, squash and of course tennis in the intervening time between school and entering the convent it somehow did not grab me as it had done previously so I hardly noticed its absence. (In retrospect I can see my body was affected as the weight went on.)

The penitential practices now seem somewhat bizarre but at the time I took them as part of the package. For instance, sometime during that year, we were called into Mother Mary Vincent's office (the then mistress of novices) and given a brief talk, while the contents of small blue bag were presented to us. In it was a chain with spikes on it. It was suggested you wear it some days around your thigh, tightening as much as you could bear. The other was a small rope with knots and this you were to use before going to bed, beating yourself. The latter I found fairly harmless, as it was light, but the chain could be painful if you wanted it to be.

There were two types of public penances. One was monthly, when individual novices knelt on the floor and asked the question of the forty or so others in the room: 'Dear sisters, please tell me my faults.' There was the option of replying, 'Dear sister, I observe nothing' or 'Dear sister, I observe …'. I think two or three times during my novitiate I put myself forward with the question and heard back from most of those who commented, 'Dear sister, I observe you are too independent.' My response was just to smile at the whole thing. In one way I saw that remark as a compliment. Looking back at the practice now I feel it served little purpose in the sense that I never personally experienced it as a way of improving oneself. Another more public practice was carried out in the refectory, which meant that the professed sisters were also present. You knelt, usually with another sister, at a small table in the middle of the floor, eating your entire meal in this position, then, at the end, you kissed the floor and acknowledged some fault. It was usually for something fairly harmless, like breaking something or forgetting some practice. On Good Friday, there was the extraordinary practice of eating our dinner sitting on the floor.

I should add similar practices were carried out by other congregations at the time. Vatican II changed a great deal in religious formation and religious life in general with regard to both outward practices and more enlightened views and attitudes towards what is central to religious life. There was a general cultural change in all aspects of Irish life from the 1960s onwards and this shift similarly affected life within religious congregations.

Sometime in the middle of that first year, all of us sisters and some lay people were in the chapel for the miraculous medal devotions. These were just finishing when we heard a huge crash. A great storm had blown the roof off the newly raised noviceship building. Some big lumps of lead came through a chapel window and missed the lay people by inches. As manaductress, my job was to leave just before the end of prayers to see everything was ready for supper. When I got there, a massive amount of debris had come through the skylight window and was lying all over the floor and tables. Miraculously, no one was hurt, escaping injury only by minutes.

There was a community of professed sisters in Milltown, but we had minimal contact with them. Mount St Anne's was not only the novitiate but also the head house of the congregation and so several sisters worked in administration. Others were involved in the primary and later the secondary school, the latter having been recently established. Occasionally, a novice helped out with teaching. The main outside contact, which was changed weekly, was accompanying Sr Teresa Emmanuel, who was the missioner. I remember one of the visits, made during my week with her, was to the home of someone who had just died. Sister had been called to lay her out and, as her companion, I received my first and only lesson in that sacred task. Apart from assigned tasks that took us outside the premises, we rarely went out. On the death of a sister who had reached her golden jubilee, we were asked to walk down to the cemetery in Donnybrook to join in the prayers at the graveside. Strangely, the gate through which we entered the grounds of the Donnybrook community is the same entrance I use today to reach my home. (The estate in which I now live was built on fields that the Sisters of Charity sold in the early 1980s. They used this money to rebuild the Merrion complex, which offers accommodation and a nursing home for blind women as well as the Caritas Convalescent Home.)

At Christmas, the novices were invited to Donnybrook to attend a concert put on by the Magdalen women; at the time, we did not know what we know now. The women seemed happy, at least on these occasions. I recall my surprise at discovering that several of them were intellectually disabled. I was familiar with the laundry, since we sent the Simmonscourt washing to them on a weekly basis. We also went to the convent in Merrion at Christmas, again for another concert put on by the blind adults as well as children in the school.

I feel a great sadness in relation to everyone affected by what happened in the industrial schools and Magdalen laundries and I want to devote some space to my thoughts in this area. I have reflected, and still am reflecting on it all, including how the unfolding story regarding these two institutions (and subsidiary situations like the adoption issue) have evolved over the past two decades. The role religious sisters (and brothers) played in these institutions is now being seen in a more balanced way in the sense that initially a common reaction was that almost every religious was tarred by the same brush whereas now it is more generally accepted that only some individual sisters and brothers were involved. These were either unsuited for this work, or acted in a severe way, or worst of all were those whose behaviour was criminal. The government generally accepts this view but still formally states that beyond individual acts of abuse, there was a widespread lack of love and kindness. How is that statement to be understood and interpreted?

The statement must be seen against the norms of the existing culture. As said previously, religious sisters, like families and everyone else in society, were people of their time. This meant, for instance, that words and expressions of love were, well into the 1960s, far more restricted than they are today. Now the word 'love' is everywhere; the phrase 'I love you' has almost replaced the common 'goodbye'. The same applies to gestures of affection becoming more openly expressed to the extent that little or almost no restriction is considered accept-able. The swing has been enormous almost to the point where the notion of 'specialness' inherent in the term 'love' is dimin-ished, and at times even lost. I know in our family, for example, it was only occasionally we saw our father giving our mother a peck-on-the-cheek type of kiss. I am sure other families were the same. There is, for example, a need to find a middle ground where genuine feelings of tenderness and intimacy are more truthfully and appropriately expressed.

An additional factor is connected with the words 'charity' and 'charitable', which in recent times tends to have a cold ring about it as opposed to the warmth of 'love'. This has not helped religious in particular since, for instance, my congrega-tion has the word 'charity' in its title. Also the phrase 'charitable works' was often seen in a matter-of-fact way in relation to the work religious 'did'. A remark of an African Jesuit leader, Fr Orobator, notes pertinently that the world should move 'away from treating Africa as an object of charity addicted to aid towards engaging the continent as a partner'.[34]

While I am indeed glad that the plight of children and young women in institutions came to the public eye and I have con-cerns for the many who are still suffering despite the redress contribution, which could never compensate for deep emotional wounds, I also remain bothered at the injustice that occurred in relation to the sisters and brothers who worked devotedly at the coalface in these institutions. I knew, and still know, some kind and gentle sisters who worked in these services. They were truly caring people, working at times twenty-four hours a day. For example, those caring for small children slept next to the dormitory and if a child was sick, her cot was taken into

---

[34] *The Tablet*, 19 October 2013.

the sister's room so that she could more closely observe them, and she then had to care for numerous children the next day. Dormitories could contain thirty beds or more – how does one reach each child every night in a personal way?

Accolades have been bestowed on individual investigative journalists in this area, despite their lack of objectivity, as shown by their failure to look in detail at the sisters' side of the story. I recall immediately after the industrial school news broke two sisters, both in positions of authority, were publicly interviewed and in both instances their responses were treated with complete disbelief. Even today, I sense if sisters were asked to be interviewed it would be almost impossible for them to say yes since public opinion, as a consequence of previous media reporting, has left them indelibly prejudged and therefore unable to be objectively heard. I also believe that the government, as well as most of all society at the time, knew about, as well as being sometimes directly responsible for, the plight in which some children and young women found themselves in the first place – a point which from the beginning has largely been ignored. Religious sisters and brothers, genuinely, in the spirit of their founders, reached out to try to meet the needs of these children and young women when there was no welfare or other groups ready to provide shelter and care. Such religious mostly had insufficient support, no training (there was none), and, above all, inadequate staff numbers. My present sadness is both for the woman who still suffer but also for the sisters who will possibly die with this shadow of misunderstanding hanging over them despite their having, in many instances, lived hidden heroic lives.

As I look back now on that spiritual year, I see the enormous gender gap that existed between male and female religious in the whole programme of formation. The most glaring difference was the fact that sisters were given no exposure to philosophy, theology or scriptural studies. In a less significant area, yet important in its own way, male religious played games and enjoyed a range of recreational activities, whereas the few activities that were available to the sisters tended to be almost childish. I can see also that the institutional form of living that we followed as novices had similarities to and most likely influenced the way of life that was set up in industrial schools, orphanages and Magdalen laundries. The rigidity and at times harshness of the routine, the silence, the prayers, and the minute methods of cleaning and washing with regard to manual tasks were certainly carried over into these institutions. There was one huge difference, of course, that religious chose this way of life and the strictness of noviceship life lasted less than three years. A further aspect to life, which may have been transferred to other institutions, was the practice of daily reporting about one's duties, as well as the constant asking for permission for relatively trivial things. Despite these reservations, I did not perceive my noviciate in a negative light. I truly enjoyed my time there, met many people and looked forward to what lay ahead, having briefly touched upon the many apostolates that one could become involved in as a professed sister.

Having completed our spiritual year, many of us were dispersed in our second year to outside professed houses. I was delighted to be sent to the convent in Hammersmith. Due to another large number of entrants in 1956, including my sister Elizabeth, some of us were left out longer than usual. I was nine months away and loved the whole experience. The convent was in a quaint house, almost on the Thames, with a beautiful little chapel. Similar to my time in Howth, my task was to accompany the missioner, Sr Ann Carmel, who had not yet arrived to take up her new post. I was allowed to get started in small ways and it was I, in a way, who trained her in. Sr Ann had never been out of Ireland, so many things were new to her. Crispin (John's friend with whom I had had a romance) came to visit me. We had a pleasant time together but did not arrange to meet again. Maybe we both knew that things were different now. I was annoyed though, when I heard that Mother Teresa Anthony had been told about our meeting and sent back word that he was not to visit again. I felt that should have been left for me to decide, not her.

I returned to Ireland in March to prepare for our profession of vows on 2 May 1957. Everything went on more or less the same as before, except my sister Elizabeth was now a postulant in the noviceship. She seemed to have settled in quite well, but I suppose my protective sisterly eye wondered at times how she was really getting on. Of the profession day itself, I can recall almost nothing except being presented with my ring, on which was engraved my chosen motto, 'Lord I believe, help my unbelief', and also a white apron, symbol of our fourth vow. In the days after profession, we all eagerly waited to find out our 'destination'. I discovered that I was being sent to a university in Liverpool to study social work the following September. I was happy enough; it fitted with the earlier beginnings of my emerging social conscience, but I was nervous – would I be up to it? In those days, there was no dialogue about such decisions. It all came under a rigid interpretation of the vow of obedience: you obeyed your superior since the will of God was manifested to you through their voice. Sometimes there might be a major reason to object, but the norm was to obey. After two and a half years in the noviceship, I expect individual sisters' talents, capabilities and personalities became known by superiors, so decisions were not made totally in the dark. It took Vatican II to change to a much broader and richer understanding of the obedience vow. This particular vow is central to Jesuits and particularly in relation to where they are sent on mission. In recent times I have seen the amount of thought and prayer that goes into making a decision both on the part of the superior and the individual Jesuit. Dialogue goes on at a deep level and often over a lengthy period of time. I am sure, and certainly hope, that other male and female religious congregations operate in a similar fashion.

I was sent to spend the summer in our convent in Tramore where the sisters ran a school. In the summer months sisters from other convents came there for their summer holidays. My task: to cook! I was surprised, since I had never cooked for anyone before and now it was for a community. Anyway, with help, I must have managed somehow. I recall my first morning, when a bishop came to say Mass, I produced a very black-looking fried egg for his breakfast.

I am aware that I have said nothing about my inner faith life. In a sense, I was so caught up in the externals of life in the noviceship that, and I know this may sound strange, I had, or more accurately gave myself, little time for reflection. God was obviously 'there' in my life as I entered into all our prayer activities. I cannot remember consciously discerning on my vocation – I was simply aware that I was in the right place. Daily Mass, a practice I carried out from the time I was at boarding school, was and continued to be a sustaining reality. Since my First Communion I have been graced with the knowledge that I am intimately loved by God and this has been a backdrop, or undercurrent, to my life. What began to emerge in the noviceship – or maybe it came later – was the value of St Ignatius' famous phrase: 'finding God in all things'.

7

Embarking on a Healthcare Profession

In the middle of that summer of 1957 I was told plans for my future had changed. I was to study physiotherapy at the UCD School of Physiotherapy based at the Mater Hospital. I discovered later that this was the first physiotherapy school in Europe to be established within a university. This school had opened two years before I commenced. I knew at the time that it was a relatively young profession in Ireland. The profession in Ireland evolved as follows.[35] In 1905 the Irish School of Massage was established in Dublin, most of their recruits being nurses or midwives. Over the years, and in line with developments in England, this school added topics such as electrotherapy and later remedial gymnastics. In 1942 this same establishment was renamed the Dublin School of Physiotherapy and at this stage Miss Allen and Miss Micks were well recognized names running this school, which had its base in Hume Street, Dublin. In 1957 their links with Trinity College were consolidated when university diplomas were conferred but their professional accreditation continued to be given by the Chartered Society of Physiotherapy in London. The UCD students (including myself) similarly received our professional qualification from

---

[35] See 'Hands On' for 100 Years: A History of Physiotherapy in Ireland 1905–2005, edited by Dorothy Oakley (Dublin: Retired Physiotherapists Group, 2005).

the Chartered Society in London and diplomas from UCD. The awarding of professional qualifications from London for both schools continued until degree courses were established by both UCD and Trinity and when the Irish Society of Chartered Physiotherapists was established in 1983.

I was pleased at the change and it was exciting to become part of such a fledgling profession. Somehow physiotherapy immediately appealed to me, despite my knowing little about it. Being a sportsperson, the physical side of this profession seemed attractive. It also linked in with school, where biology had been one of my favourite subjects, and this fact did give me a leg up when I began anatomy studies.

I immediately went for an interview and medical. Sr Kevin, a Sister of Charity of St Paul the Apostle, travelled over from Selley Park in Birmingham to be principal of the new Mater School. No one else in Ireland was likely to have had teacher training qualifications in physiotherapy. Two of us Charity sisters were sent, one professed a few years. That sister failed her medical, which I fortunately passed. However, I was a hair's breath away from failing to qualify by possibly not having the necessary academic qualifications. I remember there were three on the interviewing board: Dr Roden, the director of the school; a Mercy sister; and Sr Kevin. A conversation went on as to whether my school certificate was of a high enough standard. I am not sure it was, but I could see Sr Kevin wanted me accepted. (I later learned that she had been to school with the Sisters of Charity in Foxford and really wanted a Sister of Charity to be part of the next group.) The final answer was yes. In the meantime, the original sister was replaced by Sr Joan and we started our studies together in October. I have been keenly aware over the years what that acceptance meant in my life. Not only did it open the door to studying physiotherapy, but that university diploma in turn gave me a basis on which to build further studies as my life unfolded. I have always been particularly grateful for this fact, which, for a few minutes during that interview, hung in the balance.

It was decided that Sr Joan and myself would reside in the convent in Temple Street Children's Hospital while remaining part of the Mount St Anne's community, where we returned for the holidays. Temple Street meant just a seven-minute walk up Eccles Street to the school. What a busy, bustling place to live – full of life and drama like any hospital but probably more poignantly so because it is a children's hospital. The sisters' bedrooms were all on the top floor, the recreation room on the ground floor and the refectory in the basement. Naturally, all the sisters, bar the two of us, worked in the hospital. Two I recall vividly: Sr Arsenius, a ward sister, and Sr Eucharia, who was in charge of outpatients. When I think of these women today, I am in awe at the depth of their caring: they were devoted to the children they looked after and their services were called on both day and night. It was a great lesson for me of our fourth vow of service of the poor in action. I also recall Sr Gilbert, the cook, who despite her demanding job was always in good humour and very kind, and also Sr Francis Regis, the almoner, with whom I became friendly.

I settled into community life in Temple Street well enough. We joined the sisters for meals and went daily to one recreation period with them. Apart from that, we were free to follow our studies. Residing in Temple Street was a good experience in community living. It enabled me to see how the sisters combined their very active apostolic life with their prayer life and other community commitments. Also, it showed me the level of tolerance that is required when living closely with a group of woman of very different age groups and temperaments. I can recall also the sense of fun that existed, as well as practical common sense. The latter was particularly shown by the superior, Mother Baptist, whom I was told was a late vocation.

As well as having that positive community experience, my inner life of faith became both more challenged and nourished through a broader range of reading. During those years I was introduced to the works of Dom Marmion, in particular *Christ, the Life of the Soul* and *Christ in His Mysteries*. From there I moved to writers like Garrigou-Lagrange OP, who opened my eyes to the breadth and depth of the Christian faith. A consequence of this was that my faith life grew both rationally as well as affectively. During the three years of physiotherapy

training and living in Temple Street, I received the odd phone
call from Mother Teresa Anthony, who wanted to know how
I was getting on as well as making suggestions regarding my
new hunger for worthwhile spiritual reading literature.

I got down to my studies in earnest from the first day of
term, since I felt that if I did not keep abreast, I would never
manage. In our first year in college, the subjects were anatomy,
physiology, physics and chemistry. Most of the lectures were
in UCD, Earlsfort Terrace. I recall three rooms in that building.
The first was the nuns' room, a small, dark room where we left
our outdoor clothing and had the odd snack. The second room
was the anatomy department's dissection room with its pun-
gent smell of formaldehyde.[36] The great big examination room,
now the National Concert Hall, was the third room. I really
enjoyed anatomy and ended up knowing *Gray's Anatomy* from
cover to cover, except the embryology section. I did well in that
exam, getting a distinction. I am not sure what the arrangement was between UCD and the English Chartered Society of
Physiotherapy.[37] I am almost certain it was the latter group who
set and marked the papers in those days. Physiology I liked, I
got by in Physics, but Chemistry proved very difficult. Apart
from familiarising myself with the periodic chart and its list of
all the elements, I understood little else in that field.

Although our main lectures were in the university, we
frequently had to go to the Mater School. Sr Kevin was a formidable woman and kept a keen eye on how we were getting on.
She was a good teacher and drew wonderful diagrams on the
blackboard. I found her helpful, but the rest of the class thought
she was too stern and strict. In our first two years, she ran the
school single-handedly. She was then joined by Mary Curran,
who came from Northern Ireland. We were about eighteen in
the class. All had just left school except for the two of us sisters,

---

[36] It was my experiences in that room that led me a few years later to deciding to
donate my body to UCD's anatomy department after my death.
[37] Relatively soon after we qualified, the profession in Ireland became independent, forming its own Chartered Society of Physiotherapy. We received a Diploma
in Physiotherapy, but it took almost two decades for physiotherapy to gain degree
status.

and I was three years older than Sr Joan; hence, I was the senior citizen. The girls were naturally into college life in its fullest sense, such as going to hops (what today would be known as discos) in '86' on St Stephen's Green, starting new relationships, and so on. We partook in few extracurricular events, but that did not bother me. I did delight, though, in hearing about some of their various escapades. Friendships also formed between different members of the class and it was wonderful to see how these lasted over the years. (We had our first full reunion forty years after commencing our studies together. Sadly, the first member of our class, Hilary Palmer, died soon after this. Bríd, her great friend from those college days, was naturally heartbroken. It was not surprising that many married the boy-friends they were going out with when in college. Among my classmates, the one I have kept closest contact with is Geraldine Quinn. Our paths have crossed in different ways over the years and we still remain good friends.)

A significant personal event occurred during my first year. All the practical physiotherapy work was done in the Mater, where Sr Kevin taught massage. She had the most wonderful pair of hands. We practiced on each other, which meant, for the two of us, definitely being out of our habits. For movement and general exercise activities, we wore shorts that were specially made for each member of the class. It was when I was being measured for my shorts that I got a shock: my waist measurement! I was horri-fied, and from that moment on decided I had to lose weight. My method was simple – to eat less. Being a young sister living in community, I could not be too conspicuous or faddy about my eating habits. I simply decided no second helpings, eat less and especially of the high-calorie foods, and do not make any food a no-go area. So, for example, instead of a whole bar of Cadbury's Dairy Milk, I would allow myself one square. It worked. It took two years to get from eleven to eight-and-a-half stone. The good thing about it was that my appetite also lessened, with the result that I have never had a problem with my weight since. I recom-mend this method to all who have weight problems.

I proceeded in my plodding way through our studies. For our intermediate and final exams we had to travel to London for the practical examinations. Our subjects changed over the years as we moved more and more into pathology and as we did it became more fascinating. Throughout the course, I stood more and more in wonderment at the human body and how it works or, sadly, at times fails to work. It was, and is, awesome. Just before I finished, Mother Teresa Anthony called me to say she wanted me to go on and do teacher training in physiotherapy. I was taken aback at the idea of more studies and then teaching, something I have never wanted to do. I had the sense that the Sisters of Charity wanted to open a physiotherapy school attached to St Vincent's Hospital. However, as it turned out, I soon heard to my relief that this was not to be. The incident taught me a great lesson. Having lived in succession through two sets of training, namely, for religious life and physiotherapy, led me to living my life in a future-orientated way. This incident made it clear that from now on my life had to be lived in the present, in the 'now'. People were not talking about the now style of living then. This insight came to me through the event itself and from having recently read Père de Caussade sj's sixteenth-century work, *Abandonment to Divine Providence*, in which he speaks about the 'sacrament of the present moment'.

Our course lasted three and a half years, so we qualified in September 1960. On 11 May of that same year I made my final vows. This was more low-key compared to clothing and first profession and yet it was a more solemn occasion. I took the event very seriously and entered into the actual ceremony in a more profound manner. It was a commitment for life and that was what I really wanted. Some time before my final vows, the affairs of our father's estate were concluded. My share, which was similar for all five of us, was £3,900. This was immediately given to the congregation. Canonically, since I belonged to a congregation of sisters, as opposed to an order of nuns, this money was technically mine and would be held by the congregation until I died. Only then it would belong to the sisters. If I was in an order, after final profession, I would not own any money.

After leaving college in early autumn I spent the intervening months in Mount St Anne's preparing for my new career. I learned previous to qualifying that a new project was being set up by the Sisters of Charity and that the building was almost complete. It was to become St Anthony's Outpatient Medical Rehabilitation Centre and was situated on Herbert Avenue, between the grounds of the Merrion Convent and St Vincent's Private Hospital.[38] Two sisters had, prior to my studies, trained in sister disciplines: Sr Marie de Montfort in speech therapy and Sr Joseph Eugene in occupational therapy. I was to make up the trilogy by adding physiotherapy. The three of us, plus a nurse, Sr Francis Mary, and the secretary, Eileen, were the initial team of this new foundation. My few months of preparation were spent in ordering equipment for the centre: tables, chairs, desks, etc., and, of course, all that was needed to equip a physiother-apy department. I also did a lot of sewing, making curtains and covers for couches for the new department.

The centre opened in February 1961 and its medical direc-tor, Dr Jack Molony, joined a few months later. It was exciting to be a founder member of this innovative work. The aim of the establishment was to provide an active rehabilitation ser-vice to those who were recovering from injuries as well as those who had long-term illnesses, such as motor neurone disease, Parkinson's disease, stroke and arthritis. Unusually, patients came for a full day's programme and stayed for a few weeks. The emphasis was on maximising each person's full potential and this was done through gym work, individual exercises, and various treatments including hydrotherapy, occupational therapy and sometimes speech therapy.

We took about thirty patients a day and gave them a midday meal. We had weekly team meetings and in addition, on Saturdays, Sr Eugene and I did home visits, sometimes together, sometimes alone and often on bicycles. I was already comfort-able visiting people in their homes after my Hammersmith and Howth experiences. Now the emphasis was on seeing firsthand how people's disability hindered their lifestyle at home. The purpose of the visit was to see what could be done to improve

---

[38] The new St Vincent's Private Hospital is now built on this site.

their situation and to assess how the family were coping with their difficulties.

A new community foundation was made to house us four sisters, plus two others who had other jobs. There is a sense of euphoria that goes with establishing both a new community and a new apostolate and I got very caught up in all of that. There was already a house in the grounds of the rehabilitation centre, and with some modifications it became a suitable convent for six sisters. For the first few years, the two front first-floor rooms were each divided into three cubicles for the six of us, which meant a very small space for each person. At that stage this did not bother me. There was a beautiful little oratory, with church furniture designed by Kenny's, established in what I suppose would have been the sitting room. It was a prayerful space and apart from community prayer times, I liked spending quiet time there on Sunday evenings. We were very blest in having appointed a newly ordained priest as chaplain, Fr Con. He had a lovely voice, as did Sr Eugene, so we always had beautiful singing at our liturgies. I tried accompanying them occasionally on the harmonium. My piano lessons bore some fruit, but I was not really good enough to do it regularly. I remember at some stage, Con lent me the notes on the Trinity he was given at Clonliffe. This really led me into deep theological waters and left me thirsting for more.

Regular Sisters of Charity community life was immediately set into motion when we all arrived on 5 February 1961. I vividly recall Sr Eugene and myself leaving Mount St Anne's on foot and walking from there to Herbert Avenue, Merrion, to our new home. Unlike the others, it was the beginning of my apostolic work in earnest. In lay language, it was my first real job. For me, work never became a separate entity as I sense it is for some people. Life was all apiece and it remained that way all my working life.

Since I was newly qualified and another physiotherapist was needed, Marie O'Donoghue was asked to leave Cappagh for one year to work with us. By the end of the first year I was in charge and over the first three years we ended up with five physiotherapists, so I quickly moved from senior to a superintendent position. The position did not matter from a salary point of view, since no sister working in the health services received a salary. Hence throughout my time as a physiotherapist within the congregation I was never paid. It was different for sisters who were teachers – they received a full salary from the government. Work in the centre grew rapidly as referring doctors got to know what the place was offering. An efficient, yet happy and relaxed, atmosphere permeated the place. In addition to the patients who followed the day's programme, the physio- therapy department was open to private patients in the early morning and late afternoon. This was largely for sports inju- ries, often people known to Dr Molony, who was part of the rugby world.

I saw more of my family, especially my mother, who lived just down the road and was also on the fundraising commit- tee for the centre. There was no question, however, of going home. For example, when my sister Bridget got married in Merrion Road church, we were not allowed to attend the cer- emony. Instead my sister Elizabeth and I were told we could watch them emerging from the church from Madonna House, then situated across the road.[39] The night before the wedding, sense seem to have prevailed and we got a message from the head house to say we could actually participate in the wedding ceremony *inside* the church.

Those first four years were an idyllic time. Work in the centre was growing from strength to strength and was personally very fulfilling. I think everyone's first job influences us greatly and both affects and effects all our future work. One key rehabilita- tion principle became embedded in me: *Do not do something for someone that they can do themselves, but do help someone when they need help,* and I add, in the latter case, *anticipate their need for help so that they do not have to ask for assistance.* This first job also gave me a great affinity for those suffering from chronic as opposed to acute illnesses. The preference to work with chronically ill people remained with me over my physiotherapy career. From the start I was aware of the need to keep up to date in my

---

[39] Now Carew House, part of St Vincent's Hospital.

profession, so if there were suitable courses I tried to participate in these if at all possible. The need for updating skills and for ongoing education in general I have always seen as important.

Community life was also happy. I was given the role of sacristan, which was not an onerous task, but one that I valued nevertheless. I have always been conscious of the need for talks, events or whatever I thought would be helpful in nourishing my spiritual life. The superior often arranged for a priest to come and give lectures every few months, and many of these were inspirational. The priest usually left himself available if sisters wanted to see him privately, and I sometimes availed of this opportunity. In one case, when I did, I experienced what I would term inappropriate behaviour, but remained silent about it. I was also introduced during that time to periodicals like *The Furrow* and *Doctrine and Life*, both of which have remained life-long 'friends'. A daily newspaper was available and, after our second year, a television appeared in the community room. I particularly remember staying up late one night to watch Neil Armstrong take his first step on the surface of the moon. Sisters also started driving cars and so I renewed my licence, one that included driving a minibus. Then, out of the blue, a call came through from Mother Teresa Anthony, saying she wanted to see me. This call was to change my life.

8

Rome

The call to the head house brought with it a totally outlandish request. Mother Teresa Anthony said she would like another sister and I to study theology in Rome on a three-year programme. She had previously asked Sr Alphonsus (later known as Sr Katherine) from the teaching profession and chose me as someone working in healthcare. I was truly aghast. Sr Alphonsus was twenty years my senior and a well-known and respected teacher. My old thinking kicked in: I did not have the brains for that kind of study. Mother Teresa Anthony also talked about her reasons for sending two sisters on this course: it would be to enhance the present formation programme and might lead to me becoming novice mistress. While I would have liked working in formation, the intellectual demands of such study would definitely be beyond me. The conversation went on, but I ended up refusing her request and off I went to my comfortable, happy place back in St Anthony's. However, I did not sleep that night. Something kept telling me that I had made a wrong decision; that I should have said yes. So the next morning I phoned Mother Teresa Anthony, aware that by this time she might have asked someone else. I noted the relief I felt when I discovered no one had been contacted, and she immediately accepted my altered way of thinking.

That meeting must have taken place around June of 1964. The course started in October. The Second Vatican Council had opened in 1962 and was facing into its third session. What an amazing time to be in Rome! I had already familiarised myself with the first Council Constitution, promulgated on the reform of the liturgy, and had been excited by what I read. First of all, the fresh new language of the document and then its content, such as vernacular in the liturgy, the priest facing the people … and it even went into things like church architecture and furnishings. Something new was in the air. (Coincidentally, or providentially, I am actually commencing this chapter of my story on 11 October 2012, the fiftieth anniversary of the opening of Vatican II.) The summer went by and I said my goodbyes to staff, patients (including patients who left, but who came back for monthly social evenings) and community. I had become so much involved and part of the place that I found it difficult to leave, especially thinking then that I would not be back there again.

With the above ties cut, Sr Alphonsus and I set off for Rome on an Alitalia flight. Arrangements had been made for us to stay in a hostel run by the Sisters of St Joseph of Cuppertino, whose premises housed both a school and a hostel. It was a big building on a beautiful site overlooking the Vatican Gardens. The hostel took in about twenty sisters, five of us from Ireland and the rest from other countries such as Hungary, Korea, China, Australia, England and Canada, so it was quite a cosmopolitan set up. English was our common language. I did briefly try to learn Italian but soon gave it up with my poor ear for languages. It was also not necessary, since English was the language of our studies and also in the hostel.

We arrived a few days before college opened. The college, Regina Mundi, had been set up a couple of years earlier by Vatican instigation and its president was a Jesuit, Fr Dezza. Its purpose was to offer a theological programme of studies to religious sisters from around the world and it was divided into four language sections. The biggest was English-speaking, then French, Italian and Spanish. A kindly Holy Child sister, Mother Basil, was in charge of our section.

As with my earlier physiotherapy studies I immediately got down to studying, in this instance even before term began. But study what? I decided to read the social encyclicals. This proved difficult, not having ever read a full encyclical before, and having no one to guide me. However, when term did begin, everything took off. I was hungry for theological nourishment and received with joy and excitement all that was offered over the next three years. I took copious notes at each lecture, went over these every evening and tried to do some of the suggested reading. It was the first time I had ever delved into books in a library. One row of books I clearly remember. They were a Migne set of the writings of the early fathers of the Church starting with St Ignatius (second century) up to St Augustine (fifth century). I was enthralled with all that was available, and particularly the discovery of the rich heritage contained in these works of the early church fathers.

I am hazy about the subjects we covered. The principal ones were dogma (taught by a friendly Irish Dominican, Fr Ryan), scripture (lecturers changed, depending whether it was on Old Testament, the Gospels or St Paul), moral theology, psychology (Fr Seán O'Riordan, an Irish Redemptorist) and Church history. The latter I found, at the time, the least interesting. However, I later appreciated it far more, as I realised how essential history is in enabling us to understand how life and culture evolved to our experience of living in today's world – in both its secular and religious dimensions. Lectures filled the entire morning. It took about fifteen minutes to walk from the hostel to college, the route being around the outside of the Vatican walls. When the Council was in session during our first term, we got out just in time and were close enough to St Peter's Square to see a sea of red and purple as the 4,000 or so Council Fathers came down the steps of the basilica to meet their waiting buses. It was a tremendous sight. This we did most mornings, because we also learned early on that the Council press office was located near the square where they distributed English-language press handouts of the happenings of the day before.

Being there during the Council added great excitement to our time in Rome. Three particular events stand out. Firstly, some of the well-known theologians gave talks on certain evenings, some in English. I remember in particular hearing Schillebeeckx speak. A second highlight was the Masses held in the Jesuit Curia on Borgo Sancto Spiritu at 5 p.m. each evening. These were organised by two great Irish journalists who were reporting on the Council, Louis McRedmond and Seán Mac Réamoinn. These Masses were aimed at the Irish community who lived in Rome at that time. It was my first experience of the new Eucharistic liturgy: prayers in English (with a bit of Irish thrown in), bidding prayers and the priest facing us. The third event was the ceremony in St Peter's on 8 December 1965 to mark the closing of the fourth and final session of the Council. This occasion included the promulgation of the last few documents, including two Constitutions, one on the Church in the Modern World and the other on Revelation and the much-debated Declaration on Religious Liberty. How much of the new teaching filtered through into our courses is impossible to say. I know I got a copy of the Vatican Documents (Abbott version) as soon as it came out in 1966. In the following couple of years I came to know the content of these documents extremely well.

Our time in Rome was not all about study, and, as I did in Paris, I managed to visit most of the significant spots in the city. During Lent in our second year I went to Mass every morning to the station church of the day. Present-day missals no longer mention these station churches, but it was an established practice over many centuries. It was, for me, a lovely way to see and pray in these very ancient churches as dawn was breaking, despite the fact it meant getting up at 5.30 a.m. to get the first tram to wherever the church was. In total, I must have visited over 25 different churches. San Clemente, one of the oldest churches in Rome, became one of my favourites. I particularly liked its apse mosaic, whose subject matter was the tree of life. I became very familiar with the four major basilicas: St Peter's, Mary Major, John Lateran and St Paul's. St Paul's was, in a way, my favourite, although each had its own unique architecture and, above all, spirit.

Prayer life was also enhanced by experiencing it in different settings. For example, vespers were a treat in the great

Benedictine monastery at Sant'Anselmo. I remember going there in Advent for vespers to hear the first 'O' antiphon being sung. There was a smaller Benedictine monastery closer to us, San Gerolamo, where I liked to go to vespers on Sundays. It was a very quiet, prayerful spot. I also discovered the Little Sisters and Brothers of Jesus. They had separate houses in Tre Fontane and both had the marks of a life lived in utter simplicity. From this newer form of semi-contemplative life, I also visited Subiaco, where St Benedict (fifth century), the founder of western monasticism, lived. In a less contemplative vein, I became aware of the Movement for a Better World, started by Fr Lombardi sj, and went to several of their meetings. It was there that I came across shared prayer for the first time. I was astonished one day to find myself actually sharing something within the group. It was a real breakthrough.

Social life was in one way minimal and yet we were meeting people all the time. The five Irish sisters met each weekday afternoon for tea in Sr Aengus' room. She was a Mercy sister and a year ahead of the rest of us and knew the ropes well. Sr Alphonsus, Sr Maura (a Medical Missionary sister), Sr Pauline (a Louis sister) and I made up the rest. The conversation was always good; sometimes it was lighthearted but it also contained depth, normally about theological topics. Meals were also social, as we mixed with the other English-speaking sisters. I became friendly with a Hungarian woman, the first person I met who belonged to a secular institute. She, naturally, did not wear a habit, unlike the rest of us. I was grateful to her for introducing me to Ladislas Orsy sj, who helped me with my dissertation in my third year.[40]

It was in the second term when I met Sr Mary Paul and from then on we became close friends. She helped me greatly in my studies and methods of study, and a simple thing like highlighting scripture passages and making notes in the margins

---

[40] Fr Orsy sj was a peritus at the Council and as mentioned he briefly helped me with my dissertation. He became a world-famous canon lawyer and in 2014 was still giving lectures at the age of 93. I attended one he gave in Milltown Park, Dublin in 2013. It was most inspiring. The general theme was divine energy – an energy that is today very much with us and in the life of the Church in particular.

turned out to be a practice I followed from then on. She had already finished a degree in England and was a member of a French order but lived in a convent in England. We visited many places, especially those related to prayer mentioned earlier. This friendship enhanced my life greatly when I was in Rome and continued for many years afterwards.

The Christmas break was short and I smile now, thinking about what I associate with it. Sr Alphonsus was what we described in those days as 'great with the pen',[41] and during our stay in Rome she used to write letters back to the head house about how we were getting on. Snippets of these would sometimes be sent around the houses, accompanying Mother General's circular letters. She wrote, for instance, in her vivid way, about our first Christmas, describing the meal and the wine we had to drink. The latter was not approved of and we were both told by letter that we were to drink no more alcohol.

Another great joy of the Rome years was the Easter holidays. Every Easter break over the three years, John, my brother, came out for a week. I found him a lovely place to stay at the very hospitable house of the Columban Fathers. We had wonderful times together and went on various trips outside Rome, such as Assisi, which I found very beautiful. I was delighted to see the originals of Fra Angelico's frescoes – he was, and remains, one of my favourite painters – and of course, the places associated with St Francis. The pink hue of the stonework in all of the buildings was a fabulous sight, especially as the sun was setting. If I were to go back to Italy today, Assisi would take first preference. Other places John and I visited included Siena and Pompeii. John, being a Classics scholar, knew a great deal about Roman civilisation, so was particularly pleased to visit places in Rome itself, such as the Forum.

Each summer, just as most Romans did, we left the city. Ireland was, naturally, our destination. As it turned out, those summers became a very exhilarating time for me. Before we left for the holidays, we were asked to share something of what we had been given with the sisters at home. The thoughts of it,

---

[41] She wrote a very readable life of Mary Aikenhead called *A Candle Was Lit*.

at first, were terrifying. Sr Alphonsus decided she would take
scripture as her topic. I had been so enthralled in my first year
by our lecturer (I think Fr Nogosek) in fundamental theology
that I took the topic of revelation. We gave our first talks in
Mount St Anne's to a sizable number of sisters. It was strange,
but as soon as I got up to speak, all fear left me, and the desire
to share what I had been given in Rome took over. Christianity
is a revealed religion and so revelation is the core on which the
Christian faith is based. In awe, I tried to talk about the wonder-
filled reality of God who so wanted to reveal the Godself to us
that he chose to share with us what was most precious to him –
namely, his only Son: 'God so loved the world that he gave his
only Son' (John 3:16). Paul captures how Jesus in fact lived out
this happening: 'Who, being in the form of God, did not count
equality with God something to be grasped. But he emptied
himself, taking the form of servant, becoming as human beings
are; and being in every way like a human being, he was hum-
bler yet, even to accepting death on a cross' (Philippians 2:6–8).

I think both of us communicated our excitement to our audience and it was a great success, so much so that other talks were
arranged for different convent venues. In fact, over the three
summers, I saw many of the houses of the congregation in both
England and Ireland. I cannot recall what topic I chose for the
second summer, but I know the final series after completing
our course was on religious life and in particular the vows of
poverty, chastity and obedience. Again, this series seemed to go
down well with the sisters, though I did sense an unease being
shown by a few superiors when I was talking about Vatican II's
more nuanced understanding of the vow of obedience as lived
in religious life. I even remember the venue – the hall in the
convent at Merrion.

Final exams were in June. At the same time, Sr Alphonsus
had to go to hospital, so it was difficult trying to visit her and
complete exams. I need not have worried, as I did well. We did
not receive a certificate, but instead were given a booklet with
our marks for the various subjects. I was delighted. That booklet became invaluable when, over thirty years later, it enabled
me to pursue further studies. The qualification I received was a

Diploma in Theology. Two years later the same course received degree status. (History repeated itself in the sense that the UCD Diploma in Physiotherapy also became a degree course some years after I did the exam.)

An incident that occurred during my oral dogma exam has remained with me as one of the deepest experiences of my life. Fr Ryan asked me something about faith and knowing God. I broke down in tears, suddenly overcome with something that seemed to be beyond emotion. I think they were tears of intense fullness at the realisation that faith, and the certainty that faith knowledge gives, lies beyond ordinary human knowing. It was the sheer certainty of this knowing that made me burst into this outward expression of copious tears so that for several minutes I could not speak. Fr Ryan asked me no more, and I sensed he had some idea of what this graced moment was about. Later I wondered if I passed the exam, but it did not really matter as what I received was of far more value. I did hear later that I had got through.

What I learned in Rome is not easy to put into words. The outward journey is simple to write down, but inner happenings are harder to explain. I have tried to give, or at least suggest, the intertwining of both throughout this book, but it is not that easy to achieve. The main fruit of my Rome experience could be summed up in one word: freedom. I was intellectually freer, emotionally freer and above all spiritually freer. The experience and insights of my growing spiritual freedom were great, especially in the sense of that quiet inner knowing that the Spirit of God dwells within me, energising me in all my living, be it thought, word, or actions. People have often asked me from where I get all my energy – even in the physical sense – and I know its source is the Spirit operating from deep within the core of my being. If asked what was the most significant thing I learned in my studies I would say it was the realisation that God is beyond anything we can think or imagine God to be like. In other words, God is more unlike than like anything we can ever know about him. We simply cannot conceptualise God. Like the poet Kavanagh, we can only be open to 'chinks of wonder' that can invade us, these becoming available through unexpected

happenings as well as through moments of our ordinary everyday lives.

And yet our inability to comprehend God is not entirely
impossible since the Incarnation – that great mystery, in which
Jesus reveals in human terms what our God is like. Jesus' 'coming
among us', his 'being like us in all things except sin', and his
telling us that 'he who sees me sees the Father' has changed
everything. Through Jesus, every human being is gifted with
the possibility of an intimate knowing of God; a knowing that
lies beyond ordinary human knowledge. Love calls for outward
expression and so Jesus' love as well as our own is manifested in
the way we live our lives. Jesus has told us he is 'the Way', hence
his words, actions and lifestyle shows us in some detail how we
can best live in a way that is fully human and deeply loving. In
other words, Jesus came to show us, within the limitations of
living his fully human existence, what God is like: 'kind and
full of compassion', and we his followers are called to a similar
way of living. The gift of love which 'has been poured into our
hearts' (Romans 5:5) equips us with the capacity to reach out to
everyone, even to our enemies. The latter is a unique form of
loving, promulgated only within Christianity. Forgiveness is a
hallmark of the Christian faith; we are called at least to aspire to
this reality even if we fail.

The intensely rich experience of this Roman period of my life
was followed by some surprises; surprises that required adjust-
ments, as explained in the following chapter.

9

Difficult Years

The summer of 1967 began with the third series of lectures to the sisters. While this was taking place, I got a call from the head house. Mother Teresa Anthony gave me puzzling news. She thought I needed more experience of community life and had decided to send me to the United States for one year. My job would be teaching in grade school (which runs from ages six to twelve and did not require a formal qualification in teaching). I was taken aback. There had been a silent assumption, during our stay in Rome, that Sr Alphonsus would go back to teaching, but that I would move into formation, as I had initially been told. Nothing during that initial interview had hinted at this. However, I did see some merit in her reasoning about more community experience, with the added value that this was to be in the States, and so would enlarge my knowledge of the congregation and life in general. Certainly, the idea of going to the United States was a bonus, but the thoughts of teaching children made me anxious. Anyway, the die was cast, I got my visa and off I went at the end of August.

I was given permission to stay in New York for a couple of nights with Esther Woo, the sole laywoman at Regina Mundi. She gave me a bed in her flat and showed me the sights, with the United Nations and the Empire State Building being the most memorable. From there I went to Denver for a few more days to visit my sister Bridget, who had just had her first baby, Paul, my first nephew. Then I flew off to Los Angeles where five Sisters of Charity convents had been established. My destination was Los Alamitos and, in particular, the parish of St Hedwig's, where the sisters had a convent and worked in the grade school.[42]

With a few days left to school opening, I was presented with the syllabus for the sixth-grade class, which was thought the most suitable one for me to tackle. It left me with daunting feelings and these remained throughout the school year. Mother Margaret Perpetua, the superior and principal of the school, was very kind and helped me as best she could. Each week, as was the practice, I had to present to the principal a plan of work to cover that period. Sixth-grade children were ten to eleven years old and, even at that age, some of the boys in the class were taller than I was. I had to manage all the subjects except Maths, which was taken by another teacher in exchange for me teaching her Religion class. It was during that year that I discovered for the first time the meaning of a 'Monday morning feeling'. Two particular duties stand out as I attempt to recall this year. Firstly, we did not teach fire drill, rather it was an earthquake drill. The second was a terrifying ordeal. The 500 pupils always had their lunch on picnic tables in an assigned area of the playground. One teacher was in charge to keep order there for 30 minutes. We were warned that if even one child broke ranks, namely left the table, chaos would ensue. Every teacher dreaded this duty. I was truly petrified, and just about survived maintaining order. Parents were very involved in the school and I particularly got to know the parents of one child. They invited me out and took me to see the sights in Los Angeles, including Disneyland. Coming to the close of the year, each class had its party. Thanks were given by pupils and parents, but what I most recall was the perceptive remark of one girl in the class: 'Sister, I think you would be better teaching grown-ups!' It said a lot. I think I did a job that was just about adequate. However, I know I gave it my best.

---

[42] Strange, yet again I write this sentence on 16 October, the date of St Hedwig's feast day.

I visited all the Sisters of Charity convents in California and gave a few of the talks I had delivered to the sisters in Ireland. They did not go down with the same sense of excitement. In hindsight a possible reason was that it was now over three years since the Vatican Council and some of its good news had already filtered through. I drove the community car, having had to take two lessons before I was allowed to venture on their six-lane motorways. The longest drive I ever did was after school, when a few of us went to San Diego to a funeral and drove back the same evening.

The biggest positive of the year – big in the sense of its profundity and lasting effects – was a religious insight/experience. I recall the spot: I was walking alone, saying my rosary alongside an American airbase near the convent. Out of the blue, the realisation came that if the Incarnation was true, then everything else was possible. In other words, if God could imagine and then carry out sending his son to inhabit and truly live a full human existence, then everything in the Christian faith is possible. For instance, knowing that we are deeply loved and cared for in all life's happenings, that the Eucharist and the other sacraments under their particular symbolic forms really and truly make Jesus present in the here and now of our lives are also then possible. This understanding of life does, of course, depend on faith in the Christ event. My certainty, that 'God is', which came to me during my dogma exam, was thus enhanced further by this new revelation. In essence, it was a graced knowing, which enabled me to see and acknowledge more fully that the Godhead comes close to us in the person of Jesus when he lived his life in Palestine 2,000 years ago as well as in this post-resurrection era, where he promised to remain with us until the end of time. As shown in the Incarnation event, 'nothing is impossible to God' (Luke 1:38). These words, spoken to Mary at the time of her annunciation, are also true in relation to our own lives.

About two weeks before the end of the school year I went to the chapel and found a letter in my prie-dieu with Mother Teresa Anthony's distinctive handwriting on it. I knew it must have something to do with my future. Just as before, it contained unexpected news. I was to return to St Anthony's to continue my physiotherapy work. I was taken aback: I knew something was wrong yet had no idea what it was. Even to this day I do not know what brought about this change in direction. The word 'formation' was not mentioned. It was a very matter-of-fact letter – she would see me when I got back to Dublin, which was to be in a couple of weeks' time. My mind was full of thoughts. What had gone so wrong? Had it been my poor ability to teach? (I did not think this had any bearing on the change.) Were the sisters disappointed with me in some way? (I did not and do not know.) Or was it the fateful talk I gave in Merrion some ten months previously? When I recovered some-what, I opened my Bible, which was also in the prie-dieu, and came across a phrase in a psalm: 'My times are in your hand' (Psalms 31:15). It steadied me, gave me insight enough to cope and even gave some form of consolation. Going back to physio-therapy work, which I liked, did not bother me. It was just the disappointment of not moving into formation, having been geared in that direction, and also sensing that, in some way, I had disappointed the Mother General and, presumably, some of the sisters, and the fact that I was left in the dark as to what their difficulty was.

I travelled home with a bewildered heart and went to meet Mother Teresa Anthony. I knew something was radically wrong, since little was said other than she wanted me to see a priest psychologist. That really baffled me, but the appointment had been made and I duly went. I had no idea what I was there for. I had three visits, experienced some inappropriate behav-iour and left none the wiser. For something to say I did mention the idea, which I had briefly toyed with, but not in a serious way, about moving to a more contemplative form of religious life. This was totally dismissed by the priest.

I rejoined St Anthony's community after a bit of a holiday, and then went back to work in the centre. As there was already a superintendent physiotherapist employed, I returned as a basic grade therapist, which I did not mind. I do recall vividly the feeling I had as I got back into my white habit. I had been wearing the black habit for the previous four years. It jolted me in some way to realise that the change was now being put into action. I knuckled down as best I could and the painful feelings of disappointment, and of being a disappointment to others, passed over time.

Work in the centre was as busy as ever, although I noticed that the clientele had altered. There were practically no trauma cases and a great increase in those with rheumatology conditions. This was not too surprising, since Dr Molony was a rheumatology consultant. I did, however, miss the dynamism that the other category of patients gave to the place. I eased back into the swing of things as the months moved on. I have little memory of the next two years. I do recall Sr Mary Paul and I had kept up our friendship while I was in the United States by lengthy letters and when I came back to Ireland she came over to visit and we spent our holidays together in Lakelands Convent over two summers. The superior there, Mother Mary Imelda, kindly made this possible. At the time this was considered somewhat unusual.

Despite describing this chapter as the 'Difficult Years', I was never deeply unhappy. My prayer life, both private and communal, gave constant nourishment and I am sure I was still living in the afterglow of the Rome experience. In addition, there was always a sense of sisterly companionship, especially from particular sisters. From the beginning, I experienced religious life as a wholesome and satisfying way of life. Like all human living, it had its ups and downs, and I coped with the latter as best I could. I was always aware, and still am, that we must own and take responsibility for the choices we make in life. I could always leave, but that was not an option I considered.

10

Momentous Seventies

The year 1970 turned out to be significant, although I realised its implications only over time. My work continued in St Anthony's during the early part of the decade, but life within the community was changing, and at first this was only noticeable in small ways. For instance, we were soon allowed to revert to our baptismal name. Some took up this choice, others did not. I went back to Catherine, so from then on was known as Sr Catherine. Another change was our headdress. For those who wished, we wore a different cap, which allowed our hair to be seen, and a shorter veil. A third change was that superiors discarded the title 'Mother', so that everyone was then called 'Sister'. Regarding our communal prayer life, our litanies prayer was dropped in favour of the Office, when both morning and evening prayer were recited in common. This added great richness to our prayer life. Another change was that we were given one free half-day in the week to do what we wanted. The latter was not specified. For those of us fortunate to live near our homes, this inevitably meant we could see our families and I availed of this immediately. Others took longer to do so because, sadly I think in some cases, the sisters did not know what to do with such free time, or were not close to their homes. I was extremely fortunate in having my mother and my youngest sister Monica living just down the road. This soon led to us being allowed one week's holiday with our families, a truly unexpected and welcome bonus.

Early in 1970, John announced his engagement and impending marriage that summer. None of us had met Goody, his future wife. I was uneasy on hearing that Goody was divorced, as at the time my views on divorce were different to what they are now. I can now see that some marriages irretrievably break down and that in these cases people should have another opportunity to marry again. I had known that John was no longer a practising Catholic, and that over time his faith also dwindled. While I respected his decision, it remains a sadness for me in the sense of his missing out on the richness that faith gives me in the living out of my life's journey. Hence, for John, marrying someone who was divorced was not a problem. I wanted to meet John and simply talk over what was happening, and also meet Goody, and was given permission to go to London for a weekend. I remember it so well – taking the night boat on Friday evening after work, arriving on the train at Euston at 5.30 a.m. and then finding my way over to John's flat in Battersea. We spent the day talking. I could see from the start that he was very much in love. I do not know if I even expressed my concerns when we talked together about his situation. The next day he took me to meet Goody, who was living outside London. The encounter was fairly brief because I had to get the boat train back to Dublin that evening to be at work the following morning. Seeing them together, I saw how John and Goody were in the romantic stage of falling in love and realised I had to accept that fact.

I came home sad, not only because of the divorce but knowing that I would no longer be the significant other in John's life. Marriage, in Biblical terminology, is the event where a man leaves his family and his father's house in order to wed his new wife. This sense of leaving by the one who is getting married necessitates the experience of 'being left' by their family members, which is what I was feeling. Over recent decades I see with great clarity that all marriages are sacred happenings, be they civil, religious or, in the case of Catholics, sacramentally celebrated. The core of a marriage, for me, is a man and woman committing themselves to each other and doing so in the form of making a public statement and then officially registering this contract. My mother and Monica went to John's wedding that August, which was held in Norway, where Goody's great friends lived. John and Goody later had two children, Katie and Claire, my first and only nieces.

Life went on as usual but not for long. Almost at the same time that John got married I went on my annual retreat. Annual eight-day retreats were always an important part of every year. A list of retreats and retreat-givers went up in the spring and each one could choose which they wanted. Names were discussed, especially those who were new on that list. I picked Fr Charlie O'Connor sj, who had given well-received retreats in Ireland to the Sisters of Charity the previous year. The dates also suited my work. On the first evening of the retreat we organised a liturgy group and I was chosen to be the person to link in with the priest concerning things such as hymns for Mass, which I duly did on a daily basis. Towards the end of the retreat, I lent Fr O'Connor a book we had discussed and he said he would read it after the retreat and return it. He came across as a kindly, shy person with an impish sense of humour.

It was a prayerful retreat and I think most of the sisters appreciated it. I do recall the last night of the retreat: I never slept. Instead I felt a warm glow coming from within, which pervaded my whole self. There were no words or insights, only this deep sense of warmth and peace, a being-more-alive kind of feeling. Reflecting later, the only interpretation that I could come up with was that it was an intense momentary experience of being conscious of the Holy Spirit invading my spirit, my whole person. It was different to the two previous 'revelations' and one that I could not capture in any way. The afterglow stayed for a short while – a matter of days. However, the realisation of the presence of the Spirit dwelling within our hearts has, thankfully, never left me, despite frequently my not tuning into that reality.

I had my two weeks' holidays with a sister home from the United States. Holidays, in those days, were spent in another house of the congregation. A couple of years later, I remember going to the Sisters of Charity house in Clarenbridge, Co. Galway. It was my first time to see the west of Ireland. There were four sisters holidaying there and I hired a car and we drove all around the place. At the time that was considered quite a daring thing to do.

About two weeks after returning to St Anthony's, I received a short letter from Fr O'Connor saying he was sorry he had not yet read the book, because on returning to Cork for his holidays he discovered his sister had just been diagnosed with cancer and that his mother was very frail. I duly wrote back saying I was sorry to hear his news and not to worry about the book. Then, a week later, I received another letter. By then I knew the handwriting and paused before opening it; I sensed some- thing, something almost awesome was about to unfold. The letter was longer and more revelatory. I replied, and a regu- lar correspondence was established. This was to last a year until his ministry was changed from Limerick to Dublin. Very soon we were writing daily to each other and posting the let- ters weekly. I was, and still am, amazed how well we got to know each other through those letters and how a relationship could deepen so profoundly through letter writing. We learned much about each other, our stories and also our families. We also discussed matters such as boundaries, although that word was not used, in the relationship. For instance I knew, because he told me straight out, that his Jesuit life would always come first; it was his essential commitment. I had no difficulty com- plying with this, because I too wanted to remain a sister. We also wrote about possibilities for development. For example, he wrote about his desire to work together on some form of apos- tolate. At the time, he had ecumenism in mind since he was a keen ecumenist. We did, in fact work together later on, but in another area. From my side, I shared my wanting to be open about our friendship. In hindsight, and while actually writing this, I realise more clearly that it was through the realism and depth of sharing expressed in these letters – both his and mine – that laid the solid foundation on which our relationship in the following years would grow. I also sensed over the years that our relationship became for some an instrument in furthering their well-being. It is difficult to capture what I mean when I say this. In a general way I sense that our being comfortable with each other when in other people's company enabled those gathered with us in varying social and other events to also feel at ease. At a more tangible level, when we are with others we both work imperceptively together. Charlie unselfconsciously shares his radiant and often impish presence, which frequently elicits laughter, and, if it is a spiritual gathering and appropriate, he often unassumingly shares his simple yet profound knowledge of Jesus. My input is often to support and encourage him (he is fundamentally a shy person), while at the same time offering my more practical gifts of organisation and hospitality, as well as, hopefully, concern for those present. He was never involved with me in my professional life other than if there was an individual spiritual need. I do like having him with me in the many other aspects of my life and pursuits that I am involved in. He has always been a gentle yet solid support to me and I know I am more truly myself and operate in a more alive way when he is around. These realities are, I believe, the fruit of love, love in its many forms being God's greatest gift to everyone.

At the time there was much talk about a 'third way' in relation to priest–sister relationships. I never quite knew what was intended by the phrase 'third way', but was certain our friendship ('OH': 'our happening' as we called it) was a gift and a gift that was to be shared with others. In other words, I did not want secrecy to be part of our relationship. Friendship relationships between priests and sisters have been present throughout history, even among saints – for example, St Francis of Assisi and St Clare, St Teresa of Ávila and St John of the Cross, and St Francis de Sales and St Jane Frances de Chantal. In modern times, as in the past, some people in such relationships choose to leave their religious vocation in order to marry, others to stay and break up the friendship or alternatively, as in our case, to let the friendship deepen while fully living out the commitments of our religious lives. Discernment is needed in all three situations and whatever choice is made calls for respect. Some people may choose or find themselves in situations or arrangements that are unclear or irregular, where the way forward is filled with complications and difficulties. Endeavouring to live our humanity to the full is never easy; human complexities and imbalances are inevitably part and parcel of all adult relationships.

During that first year Charlie was teaching and living in Limerick. Over that period he came to Dublin three times to attend some workshops on catechetics and visited me in St Anthony's. It was during the second of those visits that I introduced Charlie to my mother, despite her being in hospital at the time. I felt it was a good start in being open with others about our friendship and so he met some of the sisters in my community and then my mother.

In the mid-autumn of 1970 there was to be an overlap of physiotherapy staff for a period of three months. I decided this was an opportunity to do something different. I asked to work in a factory. This was not approved of but a job as a domestic in Madonna House was organised. Madonna House (a place where babies and young children were looked after while their mothers were unwell or having other difficulties) had recently moved to Blackrock so I cycled there each day and did whatever cleaning was required: floors, laundry, etc. I later discovered I was there during the time that abuse was taking place by a member of staff, but I was unaware of it. To me the children appeared to be well cared for.

In the summer of 1971 Charlie was moved to Milltown Park to work with Leslie Barber sj in the Lay Men's Retreat Association. From then on, retreat work remained his mission both with lay people and also with religious sisters, brothers and priests. The retreats to the latter group were largely given over the summer months and for some he went to England.

It was, naturally, great for me that he came to live in Dublin. Our letter writing stopped but was replaced by a daily phone call. During that year the Charismatic Renewal came to Ireland. We both became involved and went to early meetings in Kimmage and then at Eustace Street. Charlie suggested we should start our own prayer group, which we did in mid-autumn of that year. The four founding members were the two of us; Micheline, a physiotherapist working with me, who at the time was heavily pregnant with her first child; and her husband Jim. It was held in a parlour in what was called the Retreat House but later renamed Tabor House.

The group grew organically. One of the first additions was Richard, the gardener in St Anthony's. Then came Peter, a patient in St Anthony's, followed by Dick, the husband of a patient in St Anthony's. Over time others joined, while at the same time people left, and that has been the pattern up to today. Some of the existing early members who have remained with us are Ethna and Máire. We started on a Monday night and have continued on that day, so that the prayer group is known as the Milltown Park Prayer Group or the Monday Night Prayer Group. We have had several moves regarding rooms to meet in over the prayer group's 42-year lifespan. The first move was to a large room on top of the Retreat House, then to the Conference Room in Milltown Park, and from there to a Milltown Park parlour and finally to the Oratory, our present abode. Many of the various happenings that Charlie and I became involved in or initiated over the years were shoots that flowered from the prayer group. Early in the life of the group we established annual prayer days, for which we invited interesting people to give their input. Sheila, a long-time member of the group until her death, kindly offered her house for these occasions. She was renowned for her soup, made to accompany the sandwiches each one brought for their lunch.

When the week at home came in, I had such easy access to home on days off that I availed of my first free week to go on a caravan holiday with Charlie and his sister Peg, who was then quite ill. We went to Kerry, where both of them were born. I also took some day trips to Cork, to visit Peg and Charlie. The week at home meant, of course, that my sister Elizabeth, now Sr Madeleine, could stay at home when she came over to Ireland for her holidays. Elizabeth, after her profession, became a member of the English Province. She presently lives in London working at a centre for homeless people.

A change in my workplace occurred in 1973. St Mary's Hospital, Cappagh, was low in physiotherapy staff and unable to find applicants. I was asked to fill the gap as a basic grade physiotherapist. Marie O'Donoghue was the superintendent and had held that post for a number of years. It was a blow – not from the work perspective, because I liked orthopaedics, but simply because it was at the other side of the city. My extra-curricular activities would surely be affected. As it turned out, many things I wanted to do proved manageable. For instance, I left work at 4.30 p.m. on Mondays, had tea with my sister, and then on to the prayer meeting, from which I made a quick exit in order to get the two buses needed to get me back to Cappagh. I recall three particular episodes about those Monday evenings. First, I had to go each Monday to the ministress for my bus fare, but I often could not find her and those minutes were precious. The second was when I missed the last bus back to Cappagh, and did not have enough money for a taxi. I started to walk but knew it was too far. Eventually, near Glasnevin, I saw a light on in a house with a car in the front and knocked on the door. I was met by a nice lady, explained my predicament and she drove me back to the hospital. Later she became a 'friend' of the hospital. The third – a lovely incident – was the hidden kindness of Sr Raphael: every Monday night, when I got back, I found a hot water bottle in my bed.

Going to Cappagh meant settling into a new community, a much larger one than I was used to in St Anthony's. Several sisters worked in the hospital, and two taught in the Mater Christi secondary school just outside the hospital grounds. Sr Albert was the great missioner, covering a large area of Finglas, and some were retired sisters with differing levels of disability. They were a wholesome group of women, all with very different temperaments. Sr Bride was the occupational therapist and we slowly became friends, a friendship that lasted over two decades until her early death from cancer.

My physiotherapy work was interesting. It was a period when joint replacement surgery, mainly hips, was really taking off. At the time, Cappagh was one of the few hospitals with a sterile-air theatre. I also did a fair amount of hydrotherapy. There was a large pool in which the physiotherapist got into the water with the patients, unlike at St Anthony's, where we had a Hubbard tank and worked from the outside. There were five orthopaedic consultants at the time (I am told today there are twenty-two) and each had their own therapist. I was fortunate in being assigned to Jimmy Sheehan.[43] He was such a good surgeon, an innovator and a kind, gentle person.

Two family events occurred. My youngest sister, Monica, married John Bastable in 1972, and Elizabeth and I were, this time, able to enter into the full celebration. Charlie was the celebrant of the Mass. I remember preparing a booklet for that wedding while we were down at the caravan holiday in Kerry. After much thought Monica and John had decided to live in my mother's house; my mother living on the ground floor and both of them and later their three boys, Conor, Eoin and Alan, taking over the rest of the house. I think it worked out well for both parties. And then in 1975 Bridget returned from the States. Her three boys, Paul, Brendan and Jason, were young enough to quickly settle into Irish life and they made their home in Dundrum. The prayer group held their first Christmas party in that house a year later, a celebration that was repeated over many years.

My weekdays were largely occupied with work, prayer and other community tasks. The weekends proved more difficult. I did take my Saturday mornings off and usually went southside. I often met Charlie before he got involved in his weekend retreats. On some of those Saturday mornings we both took Bridget's boys for walks in Ticknock. I remember these walks with particular delight. On Sundays, I was given two jobs – to look after the hospital shop and to take in new admissions. It was there, for the first time, that I started reading the newspaper. Up to this I had been relatively oblivious to what was going on in the bigger world. I was very uneducated with regard to politics, for example.

While living in Limerick in 1970s Charlie had become involved in an encounter group set up by Henry Grant sj. He

---

[43] James Sheehan was not only a renowned orthopaedic surgeon but was passionate about healthcare in Ireland. He was a key co-founder of the Blackrock Clinic, then later the Galway Clinic, followed by the Hermitage on the west side of Dublin. Sadly his offer to build the National Children's Hospital was not taken up by the government – if it had, it would most likely be built and functioning by now.

saw their value, and decided to initiate something similar after coming to Dublin. A group of eight was formed and most of these meetings were held in Cappagh, largely to suit me. While this group did not last long, it was a prelude to what was to come a few years later. These encounter groups were based on Carl Rogers's ideas.[44]

After a few years in Cappagh, I felt the need to enhance my spiritual life by doing a serious course. I was getting more interested in Ignatian spirituality and spiritual direction. I had heard of a new course that was starting in Tullabeg, extending over eight weekends. I sought permission to go, but was refused, and was never told why. I did, however, throughout this period, attend lectures and workshops in relation to faith topics as well as physiotherapy. This hankering to do something more regarding my spiritual life persisted. I discovered an Ignatian 30-day retreat in Manresa Retreat House in May 1977, and this time I was given the required permission. I had read about the Spiritual Exercises of St Ignatius and so I very much looked forward to this experience. I knew it was a big commitment but had yet to discover its powerful inner dynamic at work. That can only be achieved by actually living through the intensity of these 30 days as mapped by St Ignatius.

The time arrived for me to go on my long retreat. The retreat house was full, which I think meant there were about 35 other retreatants. There were five directors and each of us was assigned a specific Jesuit priest. There were a few preliminaries before we all entered the great silence, interrupted only by two break days. The first week is really about easing oneself into the experience. There were four hours of private prayer each day, followed by a period of reflection on that prayer period. A daily visit with one's director was also an essential part of each day. My director was Fr Paddy Cusack sj. Mass was celebrated daily by different priests.

A strange thing happened, an aside in a way, and yet it was not a distraction from my personal retreat 'work'. I noticed by

---

[44] Rogers's most famous work was *On Becoming a Person.* He also wrote a book titled *On Encounter Groups.*

day three of the retreat how poor the chapel flower arrangements were, so I asked the sacristan if I could try to do something about that situation. He agreed. Very quickly, as the retreat wore on, I changed the arrangement daily or every other day, trying to keep in line with the various themes of the retreat. I became more creative as time went on, using stones, objects from the seashore, branches and of course leaves and flowers. It was the first time I came to recognise my own ability to be creative. Also, as the retreat wore on, during the time of sharing after the homily, people would sometimes comment on the arrangement and say how it spoke to them. I was amazed.

I am a bit hazy now, but I know I got into the dynamic of the retreat before the end of the first week. This week centres on a basic meditation called 'Principle and Foundation'. Some days were more difficult than others, especially when I felt nothing much was happening. However, I found myself faced with a major challenge towards the end of the second week of Spiritual Exercises (a stage which usually takes about ten days). During this period, the focus centres on making an 'election'.[45] This is about making a choice concerning one's future. It could be about making a total change in one's present way of living, or deepening or changing something in regard to one's present lifestyle. For some, this might mean something small; for others the choice might have a more major impact. The latter emerged in my case. As I prepared for it in prayer and by talking it over with my director, I was unexpectedly, and yet very directly, called to look at where I was in my present religious vocation. This thought simply took over. I had never seriously thought about this before and neither did I enter the retreat thinking anything major would happen. I was certain I was going back to Cappagh to continue on with my physiotherapy work. I tussled and the director held me back for a few days to see if things would clarify before I moved on.

I recall deciding to do a 'retreat within a retreat' for one day. I took myself off to a quiet area in the garden around the Jesuit noviceship building, which was empty at the time. I prayed for

---

[45] Election is a central focus of the entire Spiritual Exercises of St Ignatius.

inspiration and felt I was graced that day not by an immediate answer, but in coming to a place of 'indifference'. In Ignatian terms, this means being at peace about whichever direction emerges as the way forward. Late that evening, around 11 p.m., I went to the chapel. I found a light and took out my Bible. For no particular reason, I read the story in John's Gospel about the raising of Lazarus and the words 'Come out' (John 11:43) hit me. I was given my answer very directly through that word of scripture and took it to be true. It was startling and yet left me feeling peaceful. I remember I stayed on for a while in the chapel and then went up to the flower arrangement of the day and picked a multi-coloured petal off a tulip. I pressed the petal in my Bible, where it remains to this day. I felt it would be a good idea to live with this decision for a day, 'holding myself' before the Lord. I was not seeking confirmation, since I had received my answer, but neither did I want to precipitate into action the consequences of this decision too readily. It became clear that day it was a further call, an extension of my original vocation in some way. This call came to me in words similar to those to Abraham. The first 'Come out' was followed by, 'Come to the land that I will show you' (Genesis 12:1). Like Abraham, I was not sure what the word 'land' referred to – it could mean a place, a way of life, adopting a different world view, etc. I was, however, very clear about the first word, 'Come', and its link with the 'Come out' heard the previous evening.

During that day I was also aware of Peg, Charlie's sister. Before going into retreat I knew she was very ill in St Patrick's Hospital in Cork and that Charlie had gone down to be with her. The following morning I phoned Charlie and the sister who answered said to hold on, he would be there in a few minutes. I knew. He came and told me Peg had just died.

I had told my director the previous day about my decision and that I wanted to have a quiet day praying over the new reality my life was to take. Then the next morning, namely the day I got the news from Charlie about Peg's death, I asked my director about the possibility of going to the funeral. He left that decision entirely to me. I did go with my sister Bridget and her boys. We drove to Cork and stayed in Peg's house for the night.

Immediately after the funeral Mass the next day, I came straight back to Manresa.

I slipped back into the retreat and moved on with the flow of the Exercises. A few days later, I wrote to the new Mother General, Sr Francis Rose, and asked for one year's leave of absence. She was probably not surprised, as a year earlier she had asked me if I had ever thought of leaving. At the time, and even today, I was surprised at that remark. It made me feel unwanted. Whatever about sisters at the top feeling that way, I felt it was not true for the main body of the congregation. When she said it, thoughts of leaving the congregation were certainly not in my mind. Despite this comment I remained firm in my religious life vocation.

In hindsight, I wonder was she, and maybe some other sisters, disapproving or uneasy about my relationship with Charlie? Nothing was ever said or discussed with me. For myself I was and still am clear, that my leaving the congregation had nothing to do with Charlie – it was simply a further call from God, a call within a call.

I got an immediate reply to my letter and was told not to return to Cappagh but to leave the moment the retreat ended. Again I was somewhat taken aback. There was no meeting or conversation, even over the phone. I was sad I had to leave in that abrupt and seemingly unfriendly manner.

***

Looking back on my time as a religious, both then as well as from today's perspective, I see it as a happy and rich period of my life. It meant living alongside sisters who were committed to their apostolates of varying forms: healthcare – with its specialities ranging from acute hospitals to palliative care; care of the blind; education; social work; and in particular those who had more hidden jobs like cooking, answering the door and phone, and other sorts of housework. It also meant belonging to a congregation that reached out to other countries and continents, such as England, Zambia, Nigeria, the United States and South America. Living in community, one learns tolerance as well as the importance of kindness expressed normally in little ways. I was grateful for all it taught me about human life sensed in the lives of many sisters: prayerfulness, devotion to duty, generosity, courage … the list could go on and on. It is also impossible to state how much I received from the individual sisters I lived with as well as those I met at varying times. My life then as well as later was also privileged in coming into contact with so many people and especially through the patients I attempted to treat. How true it is that 'in giving you receive'. I was always aware of and remain to the present day enormously grateful for the training the congregation gave me in my physiotherapy studies and later my time in Rome studying theology. These two courses stood to me for the rest of my life, as did many aspects of my religious life training.

I can say with utmost sincerity that I have no regrets for the 25 years I spent as a sister. It was indeed a precious time. I received a great deal and hopefully gave what I could with generosity and love. Being in the world as a lay as opposed to a religious woman did, and still does not, mean that I left all elements of religious life behind. Some remain deeply embedded, such as the importance of nourishing one's spiritual life and seeing the value of community, in the sense, in my case, of being part of groups where some participants would not have been of one's own choosing. However, the most vital element that religious life gave me is that of service – of being a servant to all we meet in life as opposed to 'lording' over anyone. Jesus was utterly clear about the way he chose to live and relate to people: 'I am among you as one who serves' (Luke 22:27).

Part Three

CONTINUITY AND CHANGE

11

Adjusting to a New Life

On leaving Manresa, my sister Bridget kindly took me in for a short period before I found somewhere to live. The first thing I had to do was to tell my mother about my decision. Initially she was upset; more accurately, she was angry. She immediately thought I was leaving in order to marry Charlie! Telling her this was not the case mattered little. However, she soon came around and supported me in my move. My sister Monica helped rig me out with more clothes. She had already given me a few outfits for my caravan holiday and other outings. I then took off for Cork in my mother's car, which I had already been using on the odd occasion. I leaned on her generosity in this regard, as, for the next three years, having no car of my own, I frequently borrowed hers. I am sure this must have inconvenienced her at times. Monica, who was living with her, had a car, which made me feel she would not be without transport, but it must have been an imposition on her.

I spent a few days in Cork helping Charlie sort things out in St Stephen's, Peg's home. He was distributing some of her furniture to friends and kindly gave me some items, which were to be very useful in my flat. On my return to Dublin I began looking in earnest for a job. I heard that the Richmond Hospital was looking for a locum and needed someone immediately, so within two days I was back at work. I had never worked in an acute hospital before, so professionally it was a broadening experience. I took the bus to work, but cycled everywhere else. The bicycle was to be my friend for years to come, but especially for the next five years. At the end of the first week I received my first ever pay cheque. I had to get a PRSI number, as up to then I had no form of identification other than my passport. From that moment on I was fortunate to be able to pay my way.

How grateful I was for my profession: for the many other opportunities it offered, as well as providing an income. I realised that other sisters who left would not have been as fortunate as I was, both from a financial perspective and for the ease in finding work. (Teachers would have been similarly fortunate, but others less so.) I received £100 from the congregation to set me on my way. One thing I did not receive was personal contact from anyone in authority. No one, at any stage after leaving, inquired to see how I was getting on. Indeed, sadly, I am almost ashamed to mention how poorly the official side of the congregation acted in regard to sisters who leave. It appears to me that male religious orders were, and still are, better at keeping contact with the men who left, on an individual basis, as well as inviting them to functions. Women's congregations seemed to have been less compassionate in this regard. I realise that this is a generalisation, but it remains my view. I am not personally angry about it then or now, rather it arouses feelings of sadness that the congregation showed itself remiss in this area. It was arranged that I go back to Cappagh for a couple of hours to collect my belongings. During that visit I was concerned about being able to print out and distribute a letter I had written so that I could send it to every house in the congregation explaining why I had chosen to leave. My primary motivation in sending this letter was my sister Elizabeth. I did not want her to have to face conjecture that might have gone on without my explaining the nature of my reason for leaving.

With a job procured, I started looking for a flat. I looked at several, and was about to sign a contract when a more suitable garden flat on Morehampton Road came to my attention. The flat was small and a bit dark, but having the garden made up for all of that. I was to live happily there for the next twelve years.

In the meantime, I was looking out for a more permanent job. After about six weeks in the Richmond Hospital, I saw a basic grade position advertised for Baggot Street Hospital. I decided to go for it because it was within easy cycling distance of my flat, the hospital was a general hospital (but not too big) and, lastly, because I knew superintendent posts came up rarely and I did not want to be in temporary work for too long. I was again fortunate and got the job. Aileen Barret, the superintendent, was very kind to me and I soon settled in and came to love the place and the work. Then lo and behold Aileen left within the year and I got the superintendent post.

The secretary manager of the hospital, Noel Nelson, was extremely thoughtful, and early on took me aside for a chat, knowing that I had spent nearly 25 years as a sister. He pointed out that not having had a salary for all those years would need to be compensated in some way in regard to my pension. He introduced me to someone from Shield Life (now Zurich) and I took out a policy with them immediately. I also decided to save a little in the post office from each monthly pay cheque from then on. He also advised me to approach the Department of Health to see if there was any way I could claim back pension monies in regard to the years I had worked in both St Anthony's and Cappagh Hospital for no salary.[46]

I settled quickly into my new job and new home. I went to Mass (in the Carmelite Monastery at Gayfield), and then on to work, so not unlike my time in the convent. The biggest change I noticed was having totally free weekends. I worked one in four of these, but still they were largely free. Soon another of those weekends was to be taken up by a course on spiritual direction and after two years I would begin spending my free weekends outside of Dublin, but more of that later. I still had family and friends around me, which compensated for the support system that community life gives. As a consequence, I would say there was no great jolt in my life. It seemed almost

---

[46] This I duly did and after two years was told that when I finally retired I could pay back for those years of lost pension money. On retirement this happened. It took all my lump-sum money to cover this, but I was grateful to have those extra years allocated to my future pension.

apiece with what had gone before, while at the same time opening out new vistas. In my inner self I was relatively certain my decision was the right one. Yet I felt it prudent to take a year's leave of absence from the congregation. This meant I was still a religious while discerning how 'living in the world' would suit me, or, more specifically, would it be the way in which I could best follow God's call in my life.

The first major happening was a group expedition to Taizé[47] in August. Charlie and I gathered a small group of interested people – I think we were fourteen. This holiday was arranged before I knew I was leaving the convent and I had planned to use the allowed week at home for this trip. We were kindly briefed about Taizé by Ann Marie Dunne and her husband Andrew (who sadly was to die soon after at a very young age). They had both been there on more than one occasion. We flew to Paris, took a train to Lyon, then a bus ride, and finally a walk up a hill to our destination. All fourteen of us were housed in one big tent. It was a great experience except for one factor – the weather. We were told to travel light and as a result few of us (unlike the German visitors) brought suitable clothes for the many downpours. We embarked on the weekly programme that the monks suggest visitors follow. The main event of each day was morning and evening prayer in their great chapel, which was furnished solely with icons and numerous nightlights. It was an utterly simple space, which exuded a spirit of prayerfulness and welcome. I am sure it could accommodate a thousand people. The famous Taizé chants,[48] punctuated with periods of silence, formed the essence of their liturgy. On occasions, there would be a talk, and we were fortunate to several times hear their founder, Brother Roger, give some input. He was always surrounded by children as he spoke.

---

[47] Taizé is an ecumenical monastery of monks founded by Brother Roger Schütz in 1940 near Lyons, in France. Today it is the home of 100 monks from varying Christian traditions: some come from Protestant backgrounds, others are Catholic. Thirty nations are represented due to the monastery having worldwide appeal. Brother Roger wrote *The Rule of Taizé*, which centres on its celibate way of life, lived together in great simplicity.

[48] These beautiful, simple, repetitive and prayerful chants are known around the Christian world. Jacques Berthier, the brother who composed them, should, I feel, be canonised or honoured in some way for giving this wonderful gift to so many people.

In between prayer, simple wholesome meals were provided, as well as discussion groups, in which everyone was encouraged to participate. The multilingual nature of these groups I found difficult, as it meant constant translating among the different languages of members in a group. Each evening Charlie celebrated Mass for our group, out in the open air. It was to be the first of many of these types of Masses in other venues over the years. I suppose since we had initiated this event Charlie and I were unofficially seen as the leaders. I looked after the practical side of things such as bookings, travel and so forth – an experience that gave a foretaste of things to come.

That same year, I applied to do the spiritual director's course, something I had wanted to do while in the congregation. I was accepted and joined fourteen other people, all religious and some of them priests. A group of five of us drove down to the Jesuit house in Tullabeg for each of the eight weekends. Herbert Dargan sj[49] was the director, assisted by Dermot Mansfield sj. Looking back, I can see how well the programme suited me at the time. The course content was interesting and led me into literature that proved helpful for my own spiritual life as well as opening up the true meaning of spiritual direction. The practical exercises in listening and counselling techniques were also to prove invaluable. On top of that was the congenial nature of the group and the companionship this brought. The qualification given was simply a certificate of participation – something that became beneficial to me in a few years' time.

***

My year's leave of absence was due to end in May 1978. At this stage, I felt certain I was on the right path in leaving religious life, yet I sensed I should request a further year. This

---

[49] I imbibed from and am profoundly indebted to Herbert for a key insight – based on Ignatius – which I have leaned on for the rest of my life as well as sharing it with others. The insight: We discover God's will for our own personal living when we tune into our deepest desires. Discerning those desires is another matter but it does give a direction in which to turn, when, for example, the way forward in life, or difficulties in particular situations, are unclear.

was duly granted. Life continued fairly routinely for most of that year with one major exception – a two-week pilgrimage to the Holy Land led by Fr Bert Richards. Bert had been director of a renewal course at Corpus Christi in London. Charlie had done that course in 1969 after his return from Zambia and was impressed both with the course and with Bert himself. We – namely, Charlie, myself and six other people, including three from the prayer group and Charlie's then superior, Mattie Meade sj – joined their group. What an experience! The first morning, as we walked into the souk in the Old City to change money at Victoria's money-changer just inside the Damascus Gate, I was completely overwhelmed. Nothing could prepare one for the smells, sounds, colour and bustle of the place. It was teeming with people. Having never been to the Middle East before, I was completely unprepared for this scene, which has probably changed little over the years. It was a powerful way of jolting me into what life would have been like for Jesus on his visits to Jerusalem and gave more insight into first-century living than some of the churches, although those built over the sites of key events in Jesus' life were highly significant.

Bert was a great leader and knew the country, and Jerusalem in particular, in great detail.[50] We walked to most places while in the city, including climbing up as well as down the Mount of Olives on our second day. He brought us to all the major religious sites. Charlie became fascinated with the whole Temple area, and in our free time I discovered the archaeologist in him. He loved pottering in the area around the southern wall of the Temple looking for treasures such as coins and bits of pottery. Over the years, that area was more fully excavated and the original steps that pilgrims took on their way into the Temple were restored.[51]

---

[50] We recommended his classic book, *Pilgrim to the Holy Land,* to all our future pilgrims.

[51] A Jewish guide told us some years later that Neil Armstrong, the astronaut, was so impressed with the thought that these were the actual steps that Jesus walked on on his way to the Temple that he kissed them and said this was a more sacred moment than his walking on the moon's surface.

Naturally, we went up north to Galilee. We took the route via the Dead Sea and made our base in Nazareth. (Not such a good idea; better to be based near the Sea of Galilee.) Two good things about staying in Nazareth was, firstly, discovering and being able to celebrate Mass at the Little Sisters of Jesus' convent where Charles de Foucauld had lived and worked. During his lifetime these grounds were the property of a Poor Clare convent. The second was venturing in our free time to the Mount of Precipitation, where the crowd tried to throw Jesus over the brow of the hill. There is a photo of me with my feet dangling over the edge as I viewed the steep drop below.

The group was very congenial, and every evening we had a sundowner. We were all invited to contribute a bottle (bought at the duty free) to this event. This social gathering, where stories and impressions were shared and questions asked, was invaluable. This happening we copied when it was our turn to take groups, although at the time I had no idea that I would be back in that land again.

***

From a work perspective, I became more aware of my lack of knowledge with regard to intensive care and the role physiotherapists have in relation to this speciality. We did not cover that area in our training, simply because such units did not exist at the time. I requested to attend a course in this field of work and was grateful to Mr Nelson for getting permission from the hospital board. The course I chose was a six-week training programme for physiotherapists in the Middlesex Hospital in London. This took place between January and February 1979. My half-niece Susan lived at that time in London and kindly put me up. I found the course very tough, as it was all so new. A lot of it was technical, and required using mechanical apparatus unfamiliar to me and necessitated a constant measuring of things such as oxygen saturation levels. I did pass, in the sense of being awarded a certificate. However, on my return, while feeling adequate, I never experienced myself as truly competent when trying to treat patients who needed this type of acute care. I also learned from this experience that as you move on in life it is difficult to grasp knowledge of a new subject or area of expertise, particularly if you are not familiar with some of the foundations on which this newer knowledge is built.

It was good for me, however, to at least have gained an overview of what is involved in intensive care work. I was also fortunate, since at that time the number of physiotherapists in our hospital grew, so we were able to employ a senior who was competent in intensive care work. At the time, Mr Shaw, a thoracic surgeon and Dr Geraghty, a cardiologist, were key figures in the hospital. Just prior to my coming, a link between the Mater and Baggot Street was made, so that cardiac patients who needed open-heart surgery went for their operation to the Mater but came to Baggot Street for their pre- and post-operative care. In these cardiac and also lung cases, it meant there was a large amount of intensive care team work to be done, which included physiotherapy. I did play a major role in setting up a cardiac rehabilitation programme for post-op patients, one of the first at the time.

Apart from weekend work, my main workload was in the busy outpatient department. Some patients came as a result of injuries, while many were suffering from back or neck pain, or from chronic conditions. As a consequence, several patients returned for ongoing periods of treatment, so we got to know them quite well. Often patients would unburden themselves, so you had to become a good listener. (A survey done in Wales found that household staff followed by physiotherapists were considered the staff patients found easiest to talk to.) Following our assessment, we offered the usual range of treatments such as heat (hot packs, infrared, shortwave diathermy), ice, electrical stimulation, ultrasound, traction, ultraviolet, massage, manipulation and, most importantly, in most cases, exercises. A crucial item was giving patients advice on what to do, as well as what not to do, in relation to each person's unique difficulties. I took pride in not running a lengthy waiting list, even if this method was used by others in the health service as a ploy to get more staff. If patients needed treatment they should receive it as soon as possible. I worked around it in the following way: apart from some of the hospital doctors, most referrals came from GPs in the area. When pressure for appointments mounted, I would phone around some of the GPs and tell them the situation and ask them only to refer their most acute cases in the immediate future. Largely, this worked.

As my final decision about cutting ties with the Sisters of Charity drew near, I decided to take a mini-retreat, and did so over a weekend during my intensive care course in London. My choice was to go to the Anglican convent of enclosed Benedictine sisters in West Malling, Kent. Charlie had spent time there before I knew him, and had introduced me to the place a year earlier, when we were in Canterbury. The decision, in a sense, was already made. I would now finalise my call to 'come out'. It was merely a case of sending off a final letter to Mother General and this I did while at West Malling Abbey. I requested that the date of my leaving would be 11 May, the anniversary of the day I made my final vows.

I wanted a sense of continuity, as I planned to take a different set of vows. I toyed with the idea, although not too seriously, of taking the consecrated virgin route. There are several women in Ireland who have taken vows to live this form of life. Each person is assigned to an individual bishop, to whom they are accountable. He, in turn, has some responsibility for their welfare. I was not, however, drawn to this, so decided to take private vows. Making a vow is similar to taking an oath. A vow is a solemn promise, usually made to a divinity and taken for a set period of time or for life. Usually a vow is made within the context of a particular structure. For instance in sacramental marriage, two people make vows to each other and to God and for life. In my case the external structure was the constitutions of my religious congregation (these constitutions being approved by the Congregation for Religious in the Vatican in 1815). I had, therefore, to apply for a dispensation from my vows from Rome – my congregation did this for me. Private vows, as I understand them, are a solemn promise made to God but without a clear-cut external framework. The day I made these vows I made them as public as I could and did so the same day that I left the convent. How does this work in practice? My vow of poverty I attempt to live in a spirit of the first beatitude; so while owning property and things I try not to be overly attached to them. It also entails trying to share what I possess (be it talents or things) with others in a spirit of openness/hospitality. The celibacy vow is lived in the same way as I lived it when in the convent. My vow of obedience has meant taking my direction(s) in life by discerning where the Holy Spirit is directing me to go. Sometimes this becomes clear, other times less so. It does demand inner honesty, of course prayerful listening and at times a certain amount of uncertainty.

I wanted the formal making of these vows on 11 May to occur during a Eucharistic celebration, where all those present would be witnesses of this event. I invited as representative a group as possible: family, friends, people from work, the prayer group and other contacts I had in various domains. I read my new vows out during Mass and have them framed in my home as a reminder of my promises. The signatures on the vow document were from Charlie, as celebrant; Peter Harnett, representing patients and the prayer group, to which he belonged; and Sr Alphonsus, a Sister of Charity and friend, representing both these groups. Some present at the celebration may have found the event unusual (not surprising in some cases, such as Mr Solomons, a doctor and also Jewish). However, I did feel supported by all present.

I remain happy in making those vows and, despite failings over the years, I try to live within the parameters of what I laid out in them. The celebration was held in my mother's house and was, I think, a happy occasion for all. I made a dress for the occasion and decided it should be red, a colour used liturgically for the Holy Spirit.

On the morning of that day, 11 May 1979, I went to meet the then Mother Provincial of the Irish Province, Sr Killian, in the Sisters of Charity convent in Donnybrook, to 'sign out' as it were. I was also, in keeping with canon law, handed back a cheque of £3,900 – my inheritance money. It was all very matter-of-fact and quick. I liked Sr Killian, so it was all done in a friendly manner. Immediately on leaving the convent, I cycled to the Permanent Building Society's office in Baggot Street and deposited the cheque – the date was to prove significant, as explained in the next chapter.

12

New Openings

With the break from the Sisters of Charity now in place, I had dinner with my friend Geraldine and her husband Brendan.[52] Brendan was an expert on money matters and I brought up the question of rented property versus purchasing. He advocated the latter, giving various reasons. The outcome of our conversation was that I started looking at properties in Dublin. I nearly bought one in Rathmines, but my solicitor, Jim, who came to the auction with me, said £18,000 would be my limit and when it went above that value he made a firm decision to withdraw. I was bitterly disappointed, but how glad I am now that purchase did not work out. I looked at other places, but within my financial range very few properties came on the market in Dublin that had even the smallest of gardens.

I decided to look outside Dublin. I thought Wicklow would not be too far – I might even manage a cottage there, as well as holding on to my rented flat. So one day during my lunch break, I took to my bicycle and called into several property businesses in the St Stephen's Green area. I tried a few with no success, until I arrived at Lisney, where a small cottage for £18,000 had just come on the market. I said I would go and see

---

[52] Tragically, Brendan died a couple of years later, only four years after marrying Geraldine.

it at the weekend. For some reason, when I got back to work, I decided to phone Lisney to ask if many people were interested and discovered three were going down that very day. I told them there would be four and asked for directions, then hastily phoned my mother to know if I could borrow her car after work to go to Wicklow. Yes was the answer, and down I went that evening to Glenmalure, a place I had never visited or even heard of. My deepest inroad to Co. Wicklow had, until then, been Glendalough.

The lovely neighbour and previous owner of the house, Breda Butler,[53] showed me around the property. The fact that the house was south-west facing, and that the garden had a stream, made it enticing. In my subconscious, maybe, I saw its potential, but I was not aware of that at the time. On Breda's suggestion, I took a more scenic route back and was caught by the beauty of the area. Whatever happened on the way home, I made a decision to go for it, and so immediately phoned Jim to put a bid in for it the following morning at the asking price. In those days you had to have your money in a building society for three months before you could get a mortgage, and as it turned out, 11 August 1979 became a crucial date – it was exactly three months since I had deposited my inheritance money.

In August of that year there was an oil crisis and petrol became scarce. I felt I could not ask an architect friend to go down but knew of an engineer in Arklow. He vetted the building and simply said it would need more radiators. He did not detect, or never mentioned, that there was no damp-proof course. I did get the walls treated later, although unsuccessfully. In the end, I dry-lined the walls from the inside and put in concrete floors. What a treasure I would have missed if all these obstacles had been brought to the fore before purchase. I finally got the keys in September. Since the house had been vacant for some months, I began organising some basic work, such as fixing broken windows and removing a big shed. A

---

[53] This county council cottage had been built for the Butler family in 1935. Breda married Andy, the youngest son of that family, who, with his mother and their two children, were the former residents before I took over.

young man removed it brick by brick and used these same bricks to build his own shed. Andy Butler introduced me to Jimmy Cullen, a builder, who has, from that time up to today, done any building or maintenance work that was needed, as well as becoming a good friend, together with his wife, Jane. And so began a pattern that was to last many years, namely, going down to Wicklow every Saturday and returning either Sunday evening or Monday morning, leaving at 6 a.m. The early months were mainly spent stripping off old wallpaper. I only began working in the garden in the summer of 1980. My half-nephew Simon was over from England and he scythed the grass and then doused it with weed-killer. As the grass grew back, I simply kept mowing it. The treatment worked, and left me with a nice lawn that still thrives today.

From those early days to the present, the cottage has played an increasingly important part in my life. I decided from the beginning to call the place 'Shekina', a Hebrew word that contains within its meaning three notions: the presence of God, with his people, in specific places. As the eighties moved on, I became more engrossed in the garden. My first major work was to divert part of the stream into two ponds. It took me a whole winter to dig out the space needed for the water. Moving much of the earth to another part of the garden was tedious, but I persevered. I was helped by a friend, Brian, who installed valves where the water entered the ponds and, at the bottom pond, to feed Rebecca, the figure who stands elegantly with her water jug spurting water into the lower pond. Originally, I purchased my first sculpture for a dark bottom corner of the garden, but the piece was too small for that site. This original granite sculpture by Cliodna Cussen had two further moves until it found its present-day home in the garden. A gazebo replaced the site of that first sculpture, which Brian designed and built, and whose proportions are just right for where it is positioned.

Over the years I made many mistakes, but went back and changed things, whether it was the outline of a bed, the colour or size of a shrub, or the positioning of a new sculpture. My second piece, a striking work by Fred Conlon,[54] is a prime example. Firstly, Fred would not let me purchase the piece until he had seen the garden, and then he agreed. I thought it would make a wonderful centrepiece, but I was wrong. This meant getting in a JCB to move it to a slightly raised area where it sits today. (I will discuss the garden and the important role it had in my life further in the next chapter.)

As a direct consequence of my time in Shekina I began to time my Sunday lunchbreak to coincide with RTE Radio One's political programme. Through this programme, more than anything else, I was drawn into politics and became interested in not only Irish affairs but also world news. And I also began buying Saturday's *Irish Times*; it was a start, but my appetite was whetted. While during my later years in the convent sisters had started going to cinemas, theatres and the concert hall, obviously when I left I was free to participate in cultural events as my horizons widened. But it was only a few years later, as I spent more time in Shekina, that I really developed an interest in current affairs and what was happening in the world around me. Due to my garden developments I acquired a keener eye for going to galleries, in particular to look at sculptural pieces.

New friendships developed – these grew in the main from among colleagues, prayer group and the other extracurricular events in which I became involved. Among old friends, Daphne remained the constant one, and when John came home for holidays I sometimes met up with our older family friends.

Soon after leaving the convent, Bill Callanan sj asked me if I would get involved with him in a new programme called Parent/Children/Faith. The aim was to involve parents with their children on faith-related topics. This involved choosing a topic, then meeting with the parents for two sessions to educate and maybe challenge their ideas on this chosen topic. At the third meeting, the children joined them and together parents and children were facilitated in their discussions on how both parties understood the topic in question. It was my first and only time of being involved in strictly catechetical work. I

---

[54] This sculpture is on the front cover of the book.

learned much and had my first experience of facilitating group sharing/discussion. After a few years Bill left and asked me to carry on. I did so for a year but could see that the parents were well able to run the programme themselves so I soon handed it over to them.

***

Charlie had read an advertisement by an English company, Fellowship Tours, looking for chaplains to accompany groups to the Holy Land. He applied and said he wanted to bring his own group. We collected a band of twenty pilgrims and in the autumn of 1980, took our group to the Holy Land. In those early days we had to have an Israeli guide, but we stayed in Palestinian hotels in Jerusalem. It went so well that we continued to go once a year until 1992, when we began to take two groups per year, one in spring and the other in the autumn. With the Holy Land's extremes in temperature, they are the seasons most comfortable for us Irish. Our agents in Jerusalem were called Arch Tours and over the years we became friendly with David Dassa, the owner. As demand for places rose and our pilgrimage project evolved, it became a more central part of both of our lives. We advertised by putting up flyers on bright orange paper in church porches. This seemed to work, and, as time went on, word-of-mouth from previous pilgrims was an added bonus. We held four preparatory talks for each group before they left for the Holy Land so that pilgrims were reasonably well informed on practical, historical, religious and cultural matters. We also set up a group called On-Going Pilgrimage, the aim of which was to further deepen people's Holy Land experience on their return home. Amazingly, some of the original on-going groups were still coming to these meetings eighteen years later.

Our guides in the Holy Land varied; some became a hindrance in that they limited time for expanding on the Christian aspect of the places we visited. We then discovered Christians could get a licence to guide and this is what Charlie did. It helped greatly, and several years later I also got my Christian Guide licence. I got to know the land extremely well, far better than I know Ireland. Our problem was in trying to fit in all the places to which we wanted to bring our pilgrims, despite our pilgrimages lasting sixteen days. Fr Pixner,[55] a German Benedictine and an archaeologist, was particularly helpful in showing us many relatively unknown spots around the Lake of Galilee that had connections with Gospel scenes. A highlight of the pilgrimage was, for many people, our daily Eucharist. Charlie had a special feel for the various places and had his own unique way of opening up the scriptures that related to the various spots where we celebrated Mass. Often these were out of doors, so we brought all that was needed for Mass with us.

A weakness in our pilgrimages was that we did not engage more with local people, but that was impossible with the itinerary we set. We did meet lovely people, especially hotel staff (in Jerusalem we stayed in a small hotel run by a Muslim family whom we got to know well, returning to the same place twice a year). We tended to meet the same people at the various sites, who always expressed their appreciation at our returning so frequently. While aware of the tense political situation, Charlie insisted we remain open to both sides – this intractable reality was always there as a sad backdrop to every pilgrimage.

Charlie's and my roles on these pilgrimages were seen along definite lines. He was the input-giver at each site, as well as the celebrant at each Eucharist. It was the homilies at these Masses that people most remember. I was perceived as the organiser. This irked some, but on the whole most appreciated my efforts. At our preparatory meetings we set down ground rules, such as punctuality. When people experienced it in practice, not all were happy. This did, however, mean that we completed our scheduled timetable each day. Shepherding thirty to forty people over fourteen days was sometimes hard work but always fulfilling, since pilgrims were greatly enriched, which meant in turn that

---

[55] I recall his wisdom when we met him at a site likely to be Bethsaida, near the Sea of Galilee, where a blind man was not cured instantly by Jesus but in stages. Pixner just happened to be passing by and Charlie asked him the meaning of this strange miracle. He replied, 'I can do so in three words: "Illumination comes slowly."' Charlie and I never forgot these words.

we also were. To an extent, all the other pilgrimages ran along similar lines and seemed also to benefit people in varying ways.

In the early eighties a new encounter group came into existence, this time meeting in my flat. There were eight of us: a married couple, four single women (one a sister), a single man, and a priest (Charlie). This went on for about seven years, and sadly concluded when the single man left for England and, shortly afterwards, Marie, the married lady, tragically died, leaving three young children. We had all become very close and knew each other's lives in an intimate way. Personal sharings were deep, sometimes painful for the individual, as well as the listeners, but all very enriching. The meetings included two or three weekend meetings a year down in the cottage. On these we had our formal encounter times as well as celebratory meals, walks and general fun. I owe each person in that group great gratitude for their deep sharing as well as the level of caring each had for one another. What I am sad about is that over time, when the meetings stopped, personal contact just seemed to slip away. In fact, I now know nothing about the lives of Bill, Maureen and Josie, after having known so much about each other. Some form of communication is essential for keeping relationships alive. How did I let this happen? The responsibility is two-sided. I just seem to have let them drift away unintentionally and now I have no way of even knowing how to contact these people.

Sometime in the mid-eighties, the de Mello evenings began.[56] The venue once again was my flat. Charlie led people in de Mello's awareness/prayer exercises, having previously done workshops with de Mello himself. These evenings became very popular, to the extent that the flat was almost too small for the numbers who crowded in. I and several others were deeply influenced by these exercises and I have read many of

---

[56] Anthony de Mello was an Indian Jesuit priest renowned for his books and workshops. He integrated his knowledge of Eastern wisdom with Christianity and normally commenced his teachings with practical awareness exercises. In the summer months he travelled abroad, including to Ireland, but then only to Jesuits. Sadly, he died in June 1987, just weeks before coming to Ireland to meet with lay people for the first time in this country.

de Mello's books. I still use his six-part video entitled *A Way to God for Today*, which achieves what the title says and speaks to people today as aptly as it did in the 1980s. Looking back, I see how profoundly de Mello enriched my spiritual life: his wisdom, humanity and vital sense of aliveness and freedom were contagious, and his Asian background opened a door for me into Hinduism and especially Buddhism. The latter I do not view as a religion but rather as a 'science of the mind', a way of life, some of whose practices, such as 'living mindfully', can enhance Christian living. I know little about Hinduism, the most ancient of all religions. From my many visits to the Holy Land I learned a great deal about the Jewish and Muslim faiths. I am more acutely aware of the importance of interfaith dialogue, especially today when fundamentalist religious elements have led to inflicting intense harm on others while, alternatively, religions when understood and lived in their true beauty can become pathways that enhance human living as well as help create a more peaceful world.

Following on from the spiritual director's course, I was asked by two people to direct them in the Ignatian Spiritual Exercises in their daily life format. This is a big commitment for the retreatant and, in a lesser way, for the director. It means following Ignatius' Spiritual Exercises while living one's daily life. It requires a commitment of one hour's prayer daily, a fifteen-minute reflection on that prayer, and normally seeing your director on a weekly basis. One retreatant completed the Exercises in about nine months. The other had more difficulty and eventually gave up after about six months, although she did find it spiritually worthwhile.

In 1982 I decided to get a dog. I simply looked at ads in the paper and saw a farmer on the Dublin/Wicklow border had a six-week-old 'working dog' for sale. It turned out he was a black and white Wicklow collie. I took myself off to see him and came back with the pup. I called him Toby (after Tobias, the only mention of someone in the Old Testament who had a dog). I had to learn fast about food, injections, dog behaviour and so on. He was, as it turned out, a faithful companion for the next sixteen years. He slept by my bed every night and came with me everywhere it was suitable to take him. Before going to work I used to exercise him in the grounds of Muckross Convent. He, of course, loved Wicklow and I was particularly happy having him with me there for security reasons, as well as for companionship. The inevitable problem of holidays was generously solved by my mother, who took him in for a number of years when I went to the Holy Land.

***

I have not mentioned family for a while: Monica's husband John got a job in New York, which entailed their whole family leaving the house in Merrion Road. This meant too, that my mother would from then on be living alone. It was a blow to those of us left behind and naturally in a special way to my mother. Then sadly, in 1985, my mother had a stroke. She was unable to live on her own, so we organised a carer who lived in on the weekdays, and then Bridget and I took turns to look after her at weekends. It is a period of my life I feel badly about. I regret I was not around for her more. Life must have been both lonely and stressful, although we did have a lovely Christmas in 1986 (her last) when John, Goody and their two girls came over. Just over a month later, in February 1987, she became very ill and was admitted to St Vincent's Hospital, where she died in a matter of days. Fortunately I was able to be with her most of the time and fortunate too that all of us were there, including Monica and her three boys, who arrived from New York just hours before she died. We held her requiem Mass in St Vincent's Hospital chapel, with Charlie as celebrant. The day before the funeral I went with him to see the family vault in Glasnevin. It was my first time to see inside it, and I counted five family coffins, all covered in dust. I was not prepared to see it in such a state, but how could it have been otherwise, since it had not been opened since my father's death 35 years earlier? I asked some men working in the cemetery if they could possibly clean it up a bit before the funeral. Thankfully they did what I requested. It was strange seeing inside the vault and especially seeing the two child coffins. One I expected (my father's infant son) but I did not know at the time of my grandfather's child. The experience also gave me a hesitancy about being buried there myself. I rather feel I won't.[57]

As many readers will know, life is different when the second parent dies. The anchor is gone. Also, I knew the family dynamic would change somewhat, and it did. As siblings, we still remain reasonably close, despite the fact that only two of the five of us live in Ireland. Possibly, when we do come together for special birthdays or other events, these meetings become more concentrated, especially as they usually last no longer than a few days. After my mother's death, the house in Merrion Road was sold.

I am aware I did things backwards. Normally people begin by buying a car and then their primary residence, whereas I bought a country property, then a car, before purchasing my Dublin home. Had I got the car or the Dublin residence first I probably would never have had Shekina. With my inheritance money from my mother I was able to buy a two-bedroom house. I was the first in the estate to pay a deposit as well as the first person to move into my new home in Donnybrook (built on Sisters of Charity land as previously mentioned). I found it hard to leave the flat with its many memories, but I knew I was doing the right thing and that my mother would be pleased with the way I used her money.

Settling in was exciting. I was fortunate in getting some furniture from Merrion Road that went back to Simmonscourt days, and I had a tiny garden, which I managed to plant up before I even got the keys to the house. A reason for buying this particular house was its large sitting room, and also its location. From now on the de Mello, Encounter, Holy Land and other groups would be better catered for. If I had a second choice of career after healthcare I would have chosen architecture or interior design work. When stressed, I cannot concentrate on ordinary print, and instead enjoy looking at pictures, particularly of

[57] My choice would be to be buried in the earth and in Shekina. Probably my remains would have to be contained in a box as ash, or bones as in an ossuary. As mentioned earlier, I made the decision to donate my body to the anatomy department in UCD nearly 30 years ago.

modern architecture and interior and exterior designs of houses and gardens.

***

Towards the end of the 1980s I felt I should do some voluntary work and was drawn to the great work of the Simon Community. I did the necessary training and then went on weekly soup runs at night. I did this for a year and then withdrew for two reasons. Firstly, I felt getting to bed so late and being up early was not fair to my patients. Secondly, I found the rhythm of the work uncongenial in the sense that too little time was spent with those who were living rough in comparison with the time spent waiting around. I know that this was my problem and it is not to be taken as a criticism of Simon.

The workplace continued its normal pattern. However, in the mid-eighties, following a conversation with Monica's sister-in-law Liz, who was working as a physiotherapist in Canada, something changed in me. I discovered her approach to patients was more educational. All she said drew a chord in me and so I changed direction in my approach to patients, particularly those I treated in the outpatient department. I spent longer assessing them, much longer in explaining to patients the cause and nature of their ailment, and then gave time going over the dos and don'ts that would help them manage their difficulties more effectively. This meant seeing the patients for a longer period per visit, but for fewer visits. This approach applied especially to those with chronic conditions. If the problem was acute, more frequent visits were required and inevitably more intervention therapy. Around the same time, I became more aware of the need for health promotion programmes. Even today our health services are largely running an illness service, with little attention being given to promoting wellness programmes. I developed a six-week series of lectures titled 'Look After Yourself', which included topics like managing stress as well as activities like exercises, posture and ways of lifting. I ran these largely from the outpatient department, but also did some outside the hospital premises. I recall two I did in Newpark

School as part of their adult education programme as well as several with women's groups in different venues. At the time I did not see how this was enlarging my professional outlook to broader issues within healthcare generally, but as it turned out I was soon to take on some of these issues.

I always stressed with staff the need for ongoing education, and followed that principle myself. Hence, conferences and workshops have punctuated my career. In 1986, I saw the need to develop better management skills and discovered that the Institute of Public Administration was running a two-year Management Diploma for Health Service Professionals. This was run on a week-release system for twelve weeks over the two years. Mr Nelson kindly gave me the go-ahead to do the course. I found it fascinating, and meeting other health professionals was an added bonus. We had written exams at the end and I did reasonably well. Part of the course's value was meeting the lecturers, many of whom worked for the health boards, and learning about the Health Care Act of 1970, which gave an overview of how the health services were structured. (Baggot Street was a voluntary hospital and part of the Federated Group of Hospitals.)[58] As well as work-related courses I also attended lectures and workshops on interesting theological topics as well as others such as the Myers–Briggs and Enneagram programmes.

I became more interested in counselling. In many ways I was doing an element of this over the years with patients. Personal difficulties often lay inherent in people's illnesses or sense of unwellness, to which I tried to offer a therapeutic listening ear. This interest led me to attend courses. Recently I found a list of some of these: the Extra-Mural Diploma in Introduction to Counselling Skills (a two-year night course), and weekend courses on the following topics: bereavement counselling (Christy Keneally), Gestalt therapy (Isabel Blau), cognitive approach to counselling (Joan O'Connor), counselling and homosexuality (Carl Berkley), sexual abuse (Deidre Walsh),

---

[58] Other hospitals in this group included the Meath, the Adelaide and Harcourt Street Children's Hospital. These hospitals later amalgamated to become Tallaght Hospital.

psycho-sexual counselling (June Berger-Quinn), and a conference on human sexuality (Irish Family Planning Association). On these courses I met several counsellors and decided I would try for accreditation. I realise today it would be more difficult, but with a certificate showing the areas covered in the spiritual director's course, coupled with the various certificates of attendance at the above list of workshops, plus mention of the small bit of psychology done in my physiotherapy training, and my subsequent working in this field indirectly with patients, I applied. After interviews, I was accepted as one of the early members of the Irish Association of Counselling.[59] My first certification of accreditation is dated 1989, and I remained a member of this association (subsequently renamed the Irish Association of Counselling and Psychotherapy in the 1990s) until 2008. I started my counselling practice in a small way in the hours after work, and later, after finishing work as a physiotherapist, I was able to take on more clients.

Similar to physiotherapy, although at a deeper level, people revealed their story to me as their counsellor in a very trusting manner. Experiencing such depth of trust was for me a truly sacred event. Most people are naturally nervous at opening up to a stranger. I used to tell them to come for one session, see how they get on, then, if they were content, to commit themselves to three sessions and after that to have as many sessions as required. Clients sometimes asked about my method of counselling and I usually replied by saying it was Rogerian,[60] but not purely so, in the sense that sometimes I might challenge their thinking, especially in regard to the way they looked at themselves or situations and so would be moving into the area of cognitive therapy. I always begin the first session by establishing two ground rules. For myself, it was naturally confidentiality, and from their perspective I strongly suggested that they be as honest with themselves as they possibly could.

---

[59] This new professional association was established in 1983.
[60] Based on the work of Carl Rogers, a well-known American psychologist and author of the classic *On Becoming a Person: A Therapist's View of Psychotherapy* (1961). He was very non-directive in his approach to counselling.

I found this second profession humbling. I was always surprised how well the one-hour session worked. I rarely had to look at the clock, but as the hour drew to a close, I found that clients began repeating themselves, as well as feeling very tired myself as a result of listening intently while trying to be fully present to each individual. Obviously, it was more difficult to 'measure' the wellness of the client on leaving, compared to physiotherapy, but I did get a sense when a person had come to a place of greater equanimity; by this I mean that they were better able to manage their lives, despite the external circumstances often remaining largely the same. I did counsel a small number of couples, beginning by seeing each partner individually. Occasionally I took families, largely in the context of caring for a parent who had become dependent. My aim was usually to facilitate siblings to view the care needed in a more equitable way. When I first began counselling I would refer clients on to a more specialised therapist when confronted with incidents of sexual abuse. However, relatively soon it became clear that an incident of abuse would often be brought up when the counselling relationship was well established. At that stage, it often seemed inappropriate to refer them on to someone else. In the light of that, I attended an intensive course for counsellors set up by the Rape Crisis Centre and felt somewhat more competent in such situations. As I look back on my counselling career I am filled with gratitude. It is an immense privilege to accompany individuals whose lives are weighed down by deep emotional and often spiritual pain in their ordinary everyday living. Sharing their vulnerability about very intimate details in their lives requires an act of courage. It was a humbling experience when clients spoke of their personal fragility and to hear about their attempts to live as best they could when they found themselves in horrific situations.

**

And now back to Shekina developments. As I acquired several more sculptures I changed the name of the cottage to Shekina Sculpture Garden. I bought some pieces from my savings while others necessitated loans from my credit union (giving 'home improvements' as my reason for the loan). One day I came across a pamphlet regarding the National Garden Competition. I entered for the Carlow/Wicklow/Kilkenny area and to my surprise won first prize. The first of these prizes was in 1988 and I won it annually until 1993. The first visitors to the garden were family, then friends, and then friends of friends. The prize-winning success led to Shekina becoming known by the public. I have always endeavoured to make it a hospitable place, a place where people feel comfortable, 'at home'. Since the beginning I have had a sense that the place is bigger than me, that it belongs to everyone who chooses to visit and especially during the time they spend in the garden. Beauty is expansive, it cannot be 'held', contained by individuals; it is there for everyone to partake in, be delighted by.

Sometime in the mid-1990s 'nature retreats' commenced using Shekina as their base. The first one was led by Colm Lavelle sj, who had a reputation for this style of retreat. Then Charlie took over in subsequent years. The retreats usually lasted for three days and normally comprised around twelve to fifteen people, who stayed in guesthouses near the garden. Each morning everyone collected at Shekina and then drove off to different spots in the area where input was given and then time allowed for meditating on the theme developed in relation to each chosen spot. It could be a stream, a field, a bridge, an ancient church, a graveyard, a forest, an abandoned house (which led to a meditation on sin), or a nearby mountain that we climbed. Most people seemed to find these days both fruitful and enjoyable, and some returned year after year. We went out in sunshine and heavy rain, taking out sandwiches for our lunch; dinner was served on the patio in Shekina.

In 1989 Charlie and I decided to take a small group to Russia for two weeks. How this inspiration came about I cannot remember. We gathered a group of about fifteen and off we went on the weekly Saturday-morning flight from Dublin to Moscow. The only thing offered on the plane was a glass of water. Russia was then the dominant country of the USSR, although this was to change only months after our visit. Because of this, we were able to take internal flights to Ukraine (Odessa), Armenia (Yerevan) and Georgia (Tbilisi). We were greeted at the airport by our lovely Russian guide, Rita, who had excellent English (Charlie kept up a correspondence with her for several years). In addition, when we went to the different states we had their guide as well as Rita, and every museum or gallery also provided their own particular guide, which meant at times having three guides with us. This was one way of having almost full employment, which I gather they did have at the time.

Some highlights of the trip: our hotel in Moscow was a boat on the river. I recall that first evening after supper when Charlie and I took the underground to Red Square. There we saw the Kremlin, outside which the guards were doing their goose-step marching, and St Basil's Church. We were to see all of these formally later but that first evening I remember the utter excitement of just being in Red Square. The gilt onion-shaped domes inside the Kremlin were striking, and Charlie was able to say Mass in a small park within the Kremlin grounds. I well remember a boat trip along the river and an amazing evening at the Moscow Circus.

I found Moscow a more interesting and attractive city than Leningrad (now St Petersburg); however, the visit to The Hermitage[61] was very special – the palace itself had the most lavish interiors I have ever seen in any building, as well as the paintings. The crowds were enormous, almost entirely citizens from different parts of the USSR, so each guide had strict rules to allow only a few minutes to visit the set of paintings allocated to them. I did manage to buy two high-quality prints of a Picasso and a Rembrandt. The gilt of the church spires and domes again were spectacular. In Armenia – the first country to become Christian early in the fourth century – we concentrated on its rich Christian heritage, visiting early monasteries and churches. In Odessa, the highlight was a cruise on the Black

---

[61] The Hermitage, or Winter Palace, as it is sometimes known, 'has travelled the long road from a small picture gallery in the palace of the Russian Empress to a major repository of art treasures' (*The Hermitage – Guide*). It is a cross between a gallery and a museum although veering towards the latter since it contains artefacts such as sculpture, jewellery and porcelain.

Sea, and a visit to the famous Odessa Steps. I remember little about Georgia except an amazingly good meal Charlie and I had in an underground restaurant, which cost us almost nothing. Everything everywhere was so cheap, although there was very little to actually buy, and the stores were almost empty of goods, including the famous GUM department store in Moscow. We certainly witnessed people queuing to buy bread. Even the hotels had no wine, and food in general was very basic. Each evening we celebrated Mass in one of the hotel rooms. All told, this pilgrimage/holiday turned out to be unexpectedly interesting and in ways I never envisaged.

13

Unexpected Happenings

The last decade of the second millennium brought big changes on the work front. Late in 1988, rumours began to circulate that Baggot Street Hospital was to close, and the following year the real scenario emerged: Baggot Street, as a general hospital, would transfer its services to St James's Hospital, and Baggot Street Hospital itself was to be taken over by the Eastern Health Board as a centre for community services. The hospital board remained, retaining ownership. This ensured that the hospital, which was established by a royal charter to care for the sick poor of Dublin city, kept to this charter. The EHB took over the running of this new community hospital, with many of its services having an outreach dimension. Included among these services was a long-stay unit for older people, as well as a day-care centre.

Staff had the choice of moving to St James's or remaining on in Baggot Street. The majority went to St James's, including all the physiotherapists, except myself. At the time, partly as a result of my management course, and particularly after reading the Department of Health's document *Health: The Wider Dimensions*, I had become interested in primary healthcare. The excitement aroused in me after reading that document called to mind a similar experience when reading the Vatican II documents for the first time. *Health: The Wider Dimensions* spoke about a more balanced emphasis in healthcare, stressing the need for primary healthcare centres as well as the importance of health promotion, an area in which I was already interested. Sadly, its focus on primary healthcare remains poorly implemented in 2015 with, for example, primary healthcare centres still sparsely spread throughout the country. I was astonished at the time, and still am, to see the Cinderella position that the community care services hold in relation to hospital services. This situation is clearly manifest in budget allocation. In comparison with what was given to acute hospital care, the proportion of funding in the late 1980s was something like 9 per cent. I do not know what the proportions are today.

I was interviewed by a senior administrator in the community care section of the health board. She asked me, as well as setting up a physiotherapy service in the long-stay unit and daycare centre, to become involved in developing physiotherapy in the community, particularly in Dublin south community care areas 1, 2 and 3. I was delighted about this. As both services took a bit of time to get off the ground, I spent time educating myself in both areas. Peta Taaffe, the matron in the hospital, supported me in my attempts to establish a holistic approach to care for older persons in this new community hospital setup. For me, this meant visiting other types of care centres and nursing homes and attending seminars. From the community perspective, I got to know the management structure of present community services, meeting the three directors of the community care areas, and being involved in interview boards for new physiotherapy staff. I was partially given and partially took on (this distinction remained unclear) the role of coordinator and mentor. As I discovered later, the post I was asked to fill was never formally endorsed within community care structures, so over time my work became both awkward and, in a sense, superfluous. I like to think I contributed something to the early days of that new service. I learned a lot and met many interesting and dedicated people. In particular, I better understood the key role played by the public healthcare nurses.

Working in the long-stay unit and daycare centre was also to prove interesting. As well as standard physiotherapy treatments, trying to make life as fulfilling as possible for residents was an important focus. I became interested in the families of these residents and how they were managing. From the beginning, outings played an important part of the care. In conjunction with the occupational therapists and nurses, we provided one-to-one or small group outings in the locality, lasting perhaps just a couple of hours, as well as major ones, which took place three times a year. I approached the Irish Wheelchair Association for the use of their bus, which they kindly gave us, since our outings were on Sundays. Michael Saunders, our friendly driver, was familiar with managing people with disabilities. Residents, families and staff came on each outing. We brought everything with us – food, walkers, even commodes – so were self-sufficient wherever we went. Our venues varied: a community hall in Skerries, on All-Ireland Sunday (the latter a favourite as it included visits to the local pubs), Maynooth College (where we ate in the great refectory), Clongowes Wood College, a school in Bray, my garden in Wicklow (on three occasions), and, last but not least, Áras an Uachtaráin, hosted by President Hillery. This was the first time so many disabled people had been accommodated at the Áras and necessitated a ramp being built to cope with the wheelchairs.

As my role in community physiotherapy faded and my interest in the plight of families who needed help grew, I began to initiate a service for family carers. Everything evolved quite quickly. I established three centres – one on the northside of Dublin, where I negotiated the use of the conference room in Clonliffe College, one on the westside in St James's Hospital, and one on the southside in Baggot Street Hospital. With my new knowledge of community care structures it seemed eliciting the help of public health nurses would be vital. Consequently, I invited all the public health nurses and others, such as social workers and other interested organisations, to preliminary meetings (one for each area), since it was they who knew which families were struggling in their caring of relatives. I told them about the proposed service of monthly meetings and gave them a starting date. The ball was now in their court. It worked. I was particularly grateful for the helpful input of

John Morgan, a carer himself, who spoke at these promotional gatherings. (He is actually a well-known lawyer, but I myself only learned that at a later date.) At the first meeting of carers in all three venues, a sizeable number turned up. I had created a programme focusing on six different topics, with input sometimes being given by a specialist, for example a social worker on carer entitlements. Topics included various aspects of caring for the disabled person's needs in relation to their physical as well as mental health. Great emphasis was placed on the importance of the carer caring for themselves – physically, emotionally, intellectually and spiritually. A whole session was devoted to managing the inevitable stress that carers experience. Input was given, followed by open discussion. The whole project took off and seemed to be answering a real need among family carers, and meeting each other over a cuppa became an invaluable part of each evening. The programme went into a second year, in the middle of which something went wrong regarding my position. My line manager was told I could no longer do this work – that I was employed as a physiotherapist. I still did my strictly physiotherapy work; these carer meetings took place in the evening. I discovered then that this work with carers had never been officially approved at a higher level, and so when news reached them, and in particular that Clonliffe was used as a venue without their knowledge, I was banished.

Despite no longer being involved in those carer meetings, a few people from all three groups asked me to consider meeting with them. This led to a monthly meeting in my home in Donnybrook, which went on for many years, up to 2005. It stopped as numbers became smaller, when either those cared for or the carer themselves died. It became a real support group for all concerned, who got to know each other very well. I was happy that this carer service got off the ground and was, in some instances, continued by others.

Over the years I had become involved with certain organisations such as Age & Opportunity and the Carers Association, which was then in its infancy under the stewardship of Frank Goodwin. I was also one of the first members of Age Action as well as being a full member of several professional associations:

the Irish Society of Chartered Physiotherapists, the Irish Gerontological Society, the Irish Association of Chartered Physiotherapists in Community Care (ISCPCC) (from whom I received a cut-glass plate naming me as a founder member, an acknowledgement I much appreciated) and the Irish Association of Counselling and Psychotherapy. From all of these groups I learned a great deal and hopefully was also a contributor.

With time on my hands at work, something entirely new opened up: to my astonishment I was about to become an author. I vividly recall the day, when, with pen and paper in hand, I took myself off to a tiny unused room in a remote part of the hospital building and began my writing project. What helped prompt this initiative was a couple who were caring for their severely autistic child and who had attended the carer programme in Clonliffe. They found the material that I gave on those evenings helpful and suggested I write a book. I had summarised in handouts the content of each of the inputs, so had plenty of material to work with. Once I started, the material seemed to pour out onto the page with little difficulty. Even the way it was ordered, and chapter headings, seemed to spring to mind very easily. I asked Martin Tierney PP, whom I knew through the Charismatic Renewal, about a publisher, and he suggested Columba Press. I approached them and they seemed to like what I had written, as well as identifying the need for such a book. This meant, from their viewpoint, that it had market value. I recall one day when I was in the office with Celia West, my editor, and the phone rang: Celia apologised to the caller and said that she could not talk at that moment as she was with an author! I had to pinch myself when I heard that word and chuckled inside, and in a sense still do at the idea of being seen as a writer. I discovered they wanted the work on a floppy disc, so that meant getting and learning how to use a computer. I purchased a laptop and a friend, May, kindly gave me a couple of lessons. Some years later, in 2000, I did an ECDL course and got my bit of paper. I am still not proficient but get by, knowing most of the basics. I can, however, get extremely stressed when things go wrong with the computer, or, more accurately in most instances, it is I who have got it wrong. The poet Brendan Kennelly kindly wrote a lovely foreword to *Who Cares? A Guide for All Who Care for Others,* which was launched by Eithne Fitzgerald TD in 1995. The book received a fair amount of publicity in reviews in papers and periodicals, as well as being given a slot in Gay Byrne's morning radio programme. I also had the opportunity to present a copy of the book to the then President, Mary Robinson, at Áras an Uachtaráin. This included bringing a small group of those I interviewed for this work, as well as the carers who gave me permission to use their case studies in relation to those they cared for.

***

My work situation deteriorated. While I retained the title 'super-intendent', I was really doing basic grade work, to which I did not object, yet at the same time felt I had insufficient work. I was also aware that I was not being properly challenged. There was one exception to this. As a physiotherapist I had a good background in lifting techniques. At that time, due to the recent EU Health and Safety Act, formal trainers had to have their bit of paper. Hence I did a week's course run by the National Ambulance Training School in 1992, which entitled me to be an official course giver. Every employee in the health service was supposed to do at least a one-day course. I devised a very packed one-day programme and gave this over many months to most of the staff. I was also asked to do this programme with some home help groups. I enjoyed this enormously – they were all such wonderful women (there was only one man in one of the groups). The thing that surprises me about the implementa-tion of the health and safety directive, both then and now, was the almost overboard emphasis on safety and very little on the health part of the title, either mental or physical. For instance, accidents are more likely to occur when a staff member is stressed, and yet little attention is paid to this. An important tool when giving the background anatomy of the spine was 'my' skeleton. I rescued it when the nursing school closed and since then it resided in the physiotherapy department. When giving these talks in other venues, I always took it with me. Some were surprised to find a skeleton in my car. However, despite these periodic workshops, I found the days long, something that I had never experienced throughout my working life, and particularly after having had such an initiating role the previous five years. Hence I decided, as I had done previously, to use this spare time creatively and so embarked on another book.

This new book grew out of a recent opportunity – I was asked to give a short talk to the healthcare section of CORI[62] on care of the older person. Among the audience was Sr Barbara, a Medical Missionary of Mary. Barbara asked me to give a full day's input on this topic to sisters who came home from the missions for a two-week renewal programme in Drogheda. This meant expanding my thinking around this vast topic. What I offered seemed to be of value to the sisters, so much so that I was invited back once a year for the next five or six years. It was work I enjoyed enormously and I kept adding or modifying both content and form of presentation. The experience and the material used in these talks led to my second book, *Falling in Love with Life: An Understanding of Ageing*. This I wrote in the spring and summer of 1996. Again Columba Press were happy to publish this work with very minor alterations. I felt very honoured that Ken Whitaker agreed to launch the book.

Although I had intended to retire at 65, my position at work continued to be problematic and so I discussed my difficulties with Peter McLoon, my union representative. It seemed, following these talks, that I might leave work earlier than anticipated, so I started looking into the possibility of becoming a prison chaplain as I have always, even up to the present day, been concerned about our prison service. I arranged two visits to Mountjoy Prison, one to the woman's prison and a second to the men's. I then applied for a post, discovering that this had to be done through the Archbishop of Dublin. I received a firm 'no' because I was a laywoman. This led to further conversations with Peter which led to the decision to leave work at the end of 1995.

---

[62] The Conference of Religious of Ireland – an association of the major religious superiors of Ireland. This organisation is divided into three sections: health, education and justice.

I had known for some years that I was hungry for further input into the world of theology. That moment had arrived and so I decided I would attempt an MA in Theology, having received the equivalent of a BA in Regina Mundi. I approached John Macken sj, who was then President of the Milltown Institute. I remember well the Saturday morning I called to his house on Morehampton Road to present him my Regina Mundi qualifications. He glanced over it and asked me had I a second language, to which I replied 'poor French'. To my surprise and delight he there and then accepted my application, despite my being weak on the second language requirement. I was keen to start in October 1995, yet was not due to leave the health service until December. A senior doctor in the community care services advised me to take sick leave, as I had been under a lot of stress the previous few months. (During my entire working career, I had only taken two days of sick leave – how blest I have been with good health.) This meant leaving Baggot Street on a Friday and starting my studies in Milltown the following Monday. There was no time to lose.

I got back into studies easily enough, and was absolutely thrilled to discover the riches offered by the library. I had to take courses in order to gain the twelve credits stipulated, and this meant selecting six courses and writing essays for each. While this was going on, I began to think about a topic for my thesis. I knew I wanted it to be around the area of faith, and in particular the question of coming to religious faith. In those early days, while being exposed to the 'greats' in the modern theological world, I was very taken by Bernard Lonergan, to whom Ray Moloney sj introduced me, and decided to base my topic largely on his writings. The eventual title emerged in my second year: *The Role of Conversion in Coming to Christian Faith: A Study Based on the Theology of Bernard Lonergan.*

I was extremely fortunate that Jim Corkery sj agreed to direct me, as he was much in demand and already overworked. I was soon to discover that he was a rigorous taskmaster, and while I appreciated him enormously, I felt daunted by the task on which I had embarked. I recall clearly going in with the first draft of my first chapter. I had put a lot of work into it and felt it was on target. It turned out it definitely was *not* up to research MA standard. Jim did make constructive suggestions, which helped, but as I presented each chapter over the next fourteen months, in each case there was much revision work to be done. In between the thesis work, there were other essays to be written. For some reason, my best time for writing turned out to be from 11 p.m. until 2 a.m., despite my trying to do it earlier. I did manage to complete the thesis in two years. It had to go through a second reader, Tom Norris DD, from Maynooth. My award was given by the National University of Ireland, to which the Milltown Institute was affiliated. I was very fortunate in getting a grant from Dublin City Council to cover the entire course.

The content of my thesis became personally important to my own inner life. I have always had an interest in faith: What is it? Can one describe it? Why do some have faith and others not? Why do some let it slide from their awareness? The essential thing about religious faith is its gift quality. Everything in life is a gift, especially the gift of personal existence, yet faith is a unique gift. The gift of faith is on offer to everyone. However, it does require a predisposition of being open to receiving this gift. When the latter is not present, faith can be absent, often missing and yet not missed.

The question of 'coming to faith' or 'deepening one's faith' largely follows a conversion path, even if this is not clearly noticeable to the individual. I found Lonergan's fourfold 'conversions'[63] helpful in coming to understand the profound gift of God that faith is. 'If only you had known the gift God is offering you' (John 4:10) are the haunting words of Jesus to the Samaritan woman. I am deeply grateful for this gift, which I received so early in life, and am still blest with the great sense of aliveness that it consistently gives me. Its preciousness, I realise, cannot be taken for granted. Faith is a living entity, a relationship, and requires constant nourishment. There are many forms of nourishment, such as prayer, charitable acts and the sacraments. For me, coming to understand more deeply the wonder of this gift is also an important form of nourishment. Believing

---

[63] These he lists as intellectual, moral, affective and religious conversion.

is a profoundly rational act, while at the same time it goes beyond the merely rational, and involves the whole person. I found Lonergan helpful in his understanding of faith and like the way he defines it: 'Faith is the knowledge born of religious love.'[64]

Lonergan views conversion as a basic human happening that involves the whole person. It demands a new orientation, a radical turning around, a change of heart. It touches the core of our being and when authentic reveals itself in our outlook, behaviour, world view and goals. Essentially, religious conversion calls for the most dramatic of all horizon shifts and is diametrically opposed to a life of drifting. When a person is religiously converted, they become aware of God's loving presence in their lives. For some this presence is experienced as a kind of undertow that lies beneath all the activities of our lives, moving in and out of consciousness, yet known to be always 'there'. I can gratefully say that I have been blest with this undertow experience. In some periods of my life it has been more prominent in my awareness than at others. But the great grace is in the knowing that this sense of being touched by God, being supported or 'held', is always there, despite my, at times, infrequent contact with that loving presence. An image or metaphor of God that came to me and remains with me is that of a safety net in a big circus tent. The acrobats are up in the top of the tent doing their various daring antics, just as I am involved in the various things I do. They are aided in their feats knowing that below them is a safety net, should they fall. Similarly, I know that God is there to catch me should I slip on life's journey. It is a consoling and true image that speaks to me. I reread this thesis recently and was really surprised to find it so rich in content and well worth the effort I put into it. I was delighted a few years ago when a lecturer in Milltown Park said he suggested that some of his students read it since it was so clear.

While the course was the main focus of the years 1995 to 1997, I also thought more about counselling. Since leaving the health service I had more time for clients, so I decided to have my

---

[64] *Method in Theology*, p. 115.

name listed in the *Golden Pages* under the auspices of the Irish Association of Counselling. This brought me more clients, without inundating me with too many. New clients seem to come at nicely spaced intervals and often old clients might return for a session or two. Having always worked in the public health service as a physiotherapist, I still find it difficult to charge clients for their session, and work on a sliding scale from five to fifty euros. Sometimes it is difficult to know where to pitch the fee – I hope I am fair in my judgement.

Falling in Love with Life continued to do well and, like *Who Cares?*, went to a second printing. Partly through word of mouth and partly due to the book I gave many workshops around Ireland on the topic of ageing under titles such as 'Positive Ageing: Living Fully the Last Third of Life' and 'Falling in Love with Life: An Understanding of Ageing'. Some workshops lasted a day; many were spread over a weekend or even longer. The main focus of the workshops was summed up in the acronym PIES: physical well-being, intellectual well-being, emotional well-being and spiritual well-being. The workshops attempted to spell out how we are all responsible for personally fostering these levels of well-being in a balanced way and what practical steps this may require as we live out our older years.

A by-product of giving these workshops was that I got to know Ireland so much better and naturally met a great number of people. I drove everywhere – Sligo, Clare, Kerry, Wexford, Westmeath, Tipperary and beyond. And, of course, Dublin. The clientele varied: some were retirement groups, others were groups of a particular religious congregation and some were diocesan priests. I had been prepared for giving workshops, having earlier given them in relation to two other topics: 'Caring: What Does It Involve?' and 'Stress Management'. Many of the latter were given largely to carers' and women's groups as a once-off, or as a series of evening meetings. Indeed the majority of groups I spoke to over the years were notable for their lack of men. I felt sad about this. It indicated that the majority of men thought little about their retirement before it happened, resulting in them being often ill-prepared for the changes in life that this new situation necessitates. There were notable exceptions. For example, I recall my three days in Mount Melleray giving input to the monks, four days with the Christian Brothers in Sligo, and a day with the priests and Bishop Willie Walsh of Killaloe diocese, as well as a group of priests in Mayo and Kilkenny.

Twice in the second half of the nineties John Quinn[65] called on me for input into two radio documentary series he was doing about the ageing process. I had a fair amount of time on both of these programmes. In his most recent book, *The Curious Mind*, he includes an excerpt from my ageing book entitled 'The Satisfactions of the Older Years'. The former two series helped promote further my workshops on ageing and led to my giving more of these around the country, as already alluded to. These were to continue for a further decade, from 1995 to 2005. John later asked me to become a contributor to his radio series *This Place Speaks to Me*. The place in my case was Shekina Sculpture Garden. In my estimation, it was the best interview I ever gave. John had obviously heard about the garden but asked no further questions until the interview began. We simply left the sun room and on hearing the sound of running water he walked towards the stream and the interview began, he with his microphone in hand. We then strolled around, stopping here and there, and especially at each sculpture. We ended with Rebecca, hearing the water flowing from her jug into the pond. It took exactly three-quarters of an hour, the actual length of the programme. I was amazed at the timing and the ease with which he conducted the interview. He was certainly a master at his interviewing craft.

***

How full the decade of the nineties seems to have been, and yet there was more to it. Hence back to Shekina. As the years wore on more and more people came to visit the garden and when Co. Wicklow tourism decided to start a garden festival in 1989, I was approached, and after their committee viewed the

---

[65] John Quinn spent 25 years producing and presenting documentary radio programmes. *The Open Mind* had the longest run and was the best known.

garden, I was included among their list. This festival continues up to today and I have been part of the festival every year since its initiation; it is hard to believe that it has been over 24 years. In the last two years the formal festival has been dropped but gardens are listed under the County Wicklow Gardens website.

I have two types of visiting days to Shekina. The first are Open Days, usually Sundays, when people come between 1 and 6 p.m. I encourage visitors to bring picnics. The garden can be 'seen' in a short space of time, but I prefer people to get value, namely, to 'experience' the garden. This requires spending more time in the place so that they really could be fully present to what the garden has to offer: peace, beauty, challenge, etc. The second type of days I call Time-Out Days. People need to book for these, arriving mid-morning, bringing a picnic lunch and leaving at 5 p.m. These more reflective days I usually facilitate, depending on the requirements of each group. I prefer groups to range from seven to twenty people. The garden has also been used for celebrations such as weddings, birthdays and other events.

In light of how people seem to be benefiting from their time in the garden, and also in terms of the garden's future, I had the idea of 'gifting' it to the nation. Sometime in 1993, I approached the Office of Public Works about this. I dealt with a very pleasant and helpful man, Chris Flynn, who facilitated the various negotiations, which lasted for over two years. Other officials came to see the garden, one of these being Seán Casey from the Department of Parks and Wildlife. Finally, in 1995, an agreement was reached and I signed a contract (approved by my solicitor, Jim). The contract is a very simple document saying that the garden would be available to me during my lifetime and continues 'The Minister for Arts, Culture and the Gaeltacht doth hereby further covenant as follows: (i) to continue to name the premises "Shekina", (ii) to keep the premises as a Sculpture Garden.' I was delighted and very honoured by this acceptance by the State. I see it very much as a privilege. I was certainly not sure at the start whether my request would be granted. There was a more formal acceptance in 1997 when the then Minister of Arts, Culture and the Gaeltacht, Michael D. Higgins (now our President), on his last day of ministerial office, came down, saw the garden, and in a speech endorsed the takeover by the State. It was a happy occasion, I think, for all present.

Alongside the signing of the contract was the publication by Dúchas (and in its second edition by the Department of the Environment) of the booklet *Shekina Sculpture Garden*. The beautiful design of this work by Creative Inputs (for which they won a graphic design prize), with photographs by Con Brogan, was edited by Jim Larner from an original text by myself.

Following on the knowledge gained through my MA, as well as a consequence of the above booklet, I decided to write another book. In this new work, I wanted to expand in greater depth on the richness contained in the sculpture collection, since many of the pieces have a symbolic content that called for some 'unpacking'. With the greater confidence gained by my studies, and having written two books, I felt ready for the challenge. At the same time copies of *Falling in Love with Life* were running out. I approached Columba Press to do a further reprint and they refused. I also showed them my new work, *Time-Out in Shekina: The Value of Symbols in Our Search for Meaning*, but they were not interested and so I decided to publish myself. I chose Eleona Books as my publishing name.[66] It was easy enough to get an ISBN number and I approached Creative Inputs to do the design and printing. This time I chose hardback. Creative Inputs did a beautiful job. Because the book focused on the garden and the garden now belonged to the nation (!), Síle de Valera (Minister for Arts, Heritage, Gaeltacht and the Islands at the time) did the launch. Fred Conlon, one of the sculptors, sadly now deceased, and Fr Michael Rogers (who brings his own groups to the garden) also spoke. This book, as in a sense expected, got a more mixed reaction. Some found it a bit heavy, while others found it nourishing and uplifting, as well as challenging.

***

---

[66] Eleona is the name of a spot near the top of the Mount of Olives, where tradition says Jesus spoke with his disciples, and where he taught them the Our Father. Similar to Shekina, I like the sound of the name Eleona.

In 1991 Charlie took a sabbatical in Jerusalem. He stayed in the
Pontifical Biblical Institute, a Jesuit house, while following the
biblical programme in Ecce Homo Convent in Jerusalem run
by the Sisters of Sion. During that time, he wrote vivid diaries,
mostly addressed to members of the prayer group, including
an amusing description of the funeral of the Armenian patri-
arch in the Cathedral of St James. His wonderfully colourful
description brought the event alive to all who read it. During
their Christmas break I went out to visit him, and we joined a
group from England who were spending two weeks in Egypt. It
was a great experience. We visited the usual spots in Cairo, then
Alexandria, followed by a long train journey to Luxor, seeing
especially the fascinating Tombs of the Kings. It was strange
spending Christmas Day in Luxor. I remember sitting by the
Nile, eating Christmas cake given to us by a thoughtful friend,
Bairbre. From there we took a boat down the Nile to Aswan. I
found this one of the most beautiful spots I have ever visited,
especially when sailing in a felucca. At Easter, I brought out our
usual pilgrimage group and so Charlie and I met up again for
two weeks. A change in our routine Holy Land arrangements
occurred during the nineties when our agent in England went
bankrupt and withdrew their services. We immediately got
onto Sadlier Travel in Dublin, where Alan Benson came to our
rescue in an amazing way, having only a few weeks to cope
with our forthcoming pilgrimage. He was excellent and we
stayed with him from then on, delighted with his competence
and friendliness.

Throughout the nineties and into the first half of 2000, another
encounter group became an important backdrop to everything
else that was going on. The group was made up of two couples,
a sister, Charlie and two single women, one being myself. We
began, as already mentioned, in 1988 and met fortnightly, as
well as usually spending two weekends a year down in my cottage. A great deal was happening in all our lives and so life's
joys, as well as difficulties, was the source of our sharings. In
addition, in the life of this group, which continued well into the
first decade of this century, we went away on holidays together.
Two were in the south of France (where we were lent a house),

one in Canterbury and another in the west of Ireland. I appreciated these encounters and was sad when they came to an end. Each of our lives had moved on, but gratefully, in this instance, we have kept in contact with each other.

Another happening of this period was the initiating and co-leading of two other pilgrimages abroad in addition to the Holy Land. The latter continued on throughout the decade and from 1992 until 2000 became biannual. The first of the new ones was an Ignatian pilgrimage to the spots associated with Ignatius' earlier life. We were eight in total, including a friend of Charlie's, Paul Cullen sj, and a friend of mine, Phil McCarthy (now both deceased), and the arrangement this time was fly-drive plus camping. We flew to Barcelona, bringing tents borrowed from a friend. Our initial drive to our first destination, Montserrat, was quite a steep one. Here we pitched our tents in the monastery grounds – quite a job the first time as none of us were experts in camping. After a couple of days attending liturgies at the Benedictine monastery, getting used to preparing and eating camp meals, and going for walks in such a scenic place, we moved to Manresa, where Ignatius had his core religious experience at the Cardoner River and where he got the inspiration for and possibly commenced writing the Spiritual Exercises. I found the little Ignatian chapel a prayerful place. While there we went on a day's excursion to Andorra, way up in the Pyrenees. Early evening a tremendous storm hit us and the other driver and I decided we should head back. It was the scariest drive I have ever done. Our next stop was to be Loyola, the home town of Ignatius, and I was disappointed we did not make it but the group felt the drive was too long and so we returned to Barcelona. I think the Andorra experience had something to do with the change in plan. However it meant Charlie and I managed to make a return visit to Montserrat – such a beautiful and prayerful place despite the number of people who flock there. The monks share all their liturgical services with those who wished to pray with them.

A couple of years later, a group of about fifteen, mainly from the prayer group, went on pilgrimage to Iona. This time we flew to Glasgow, went by minibus to Mull and from there by boat to Iona. It is a beautiful island, and very unspoilt despite the number of pilgrims who continuously flock there. The grassland was covered with buttercups and daisies, with sheep grazing all over the island. We stayed in the guest house of the monastery. It is owned and managed by Presbyterians and functions as an ecumenical venture. Its services were Presbyterian. I had arranged for twin rooms for our group but on arrival discovered that five of the group had to share one room. I was very put out by this to the extent that it spoiled my week's experience there. As a result, I found it difficult to get into what was on offer except on the Wednesday, when there was a walking tour of the island. There were domestic chores to be done and workshops were going on all the time. To my surprise, the one that attracted me was musical composition, which I enjoyed, and I even composed a bit of music. In summary, it was an unfortunate experience, because I simply could not fit in with what was going on. Yet I realise pilgrimages are not expected to be easy affairs, and hardships of all kinds are part and parcel of 'going on pilgrimage'.

We also made two other pilgrimages within Ireland, including one to Aran. Pilgrims were largely drawn from the prayer group and the pilgrimage group, about fifteen in total. Dara Molloy led us throughout the week. I learned a tremendous amount from him about our rich religious and cultural past. Similar to the Holy Land, we celebrated our daily Masses largely out of doors in various significant spots. A few years later, in 2001, a similar group of us went to Ballintubber and were led in our five-day pilgrimage by Frank Fahy PP. The beautifully restored abbey was our focus, but we also went on walking tours in the surrounding areas, including spending a day on a small island. We stayed, as in Aran, in guest houses on both pilgrimages. Apart from pilgrimages, Charlie and I took a week's holiday in Connemara. We largely stayed with the hospitable Lydon family, who had a very remote cottage in the Maam area. Over the years I really got to love that part of the west, finding the scenery more stunning each time I went there.

***

Toby's life was soon to end. He was unwell over the summer of 1979 and I had to have him put down at the end of August, when he was sixteen. Paul, my oldest nephew and a dog lover, came with me to the vet for this sad event. We then brought him to Wicklow – surely apt for a Wicklow collie. Paul started digging the grave. The soil was powdery, soft, beautiful, having a texture I had not noticed before. We then lined the grave with a piece of hessian sacking. Placing Toby in the grave was a sacred moment. It was a giving back of his body to be cradled by Mother Earth. Before filling in the earth we had a simple ritual of thanksgiving, listening to an apt line from the Mass of the day: 'In him [Christ] were created all things in heaven and on earth … all things were created through him and for him' (Colossians 1:16) and then praying the collect from the votive Mass of thanksgiving for all God's gifts. Finally, we sprinkled his body with holy water and lowered it into the grave. The simplicity, reverence and peace of that little community farewell to Toby seemed right and proper. Just before the blessing, and out of the blue, a friend, Aline, arrived, and joined us. Thoughtfully she brought with her a big breakfast fry for after the funeral. What a lovely thought and how it added to making this event so special.

The following day Charlie came down with me to Shekina. It was Saturday, and elicited in me something of the spirit of Holy Saturday. It was a most beautiful day. I just wanted to sit in the area near the grave and Charlie joined me a short distance away. We spoke little. The bird song was unbelievably glorious, as were the other sounds of sheep, cattle and, yes, of other dogs. I became aware of our natural world in a way I had never done before and this led to a profound experience of the unity within everything that is created and the beauty and harmony of it all. I realised later that this particular grace was somehow linked with those earlier three experiences of wonder and gratitude that I previously attempted to describe. I wrote an article about the experience some months later and it was published in the Dominion journal *Spirituality* under the title 'Letting Go: Parting with a Much-Loved Companion'. It turned out this article touched animal lovers in a consoling way.

Two days later I was off to Myross Wood, in Leap, Co. Cork, on my third visit to that lovely place, where I was giving a six-day retreat using the spirituality of ageing as a backdrop. On my previous two workshops the Fathers allowed me to bring Toby along, facilitating me with a room on the ground floor. This time I was alone. This situation was not to last long as before leaving I had been in touch with the farmer from whom I had got Toby. He said he had a three-week-old collie. On my return from Cork I went to see the new pup and immediately said 'yes'. This time he was given as a gift. I did notice the big paws, so knew Andy – the name I gave to the new pup – would be bigger, which he duly turned out to be. So I was not long without a doggy companion, but this time with a dog of a very different temperament. As I write, I am conscious Andy is moving into his older years, in fact the very day I write this he had difficulty for the first time jumping into the boot of my car.

A final comment before closing this chapter: I sense that after leaving formal work in the early nineties, the way I express my life's unfolding contains less the format of story and moves more towards happenings, and commenting on these. I am not normally a storyteller. (Has this something to do with not having stories read at bedtime when a small child?) Recalling incidents and noting their significance is a format that seems to come more naturally to me. The lack of a storyline is possibly more likely as we age. A reason for this is that ageing normally entails less dramatic external changes (major exceptions being ill health or the death of loved ones). That, however, does not mean less 'movement' with regard to our inner life. The next chapter illustrates this way of writing in a more pronounced way.

14

Into a New Century

New Year's Eve, 1999. I had nothing specific organised, so I decided to see in this historic turn-of-the-millennium New Year as it began in the different countries of the world. I placed a globe and lighted candle on the table in front of me and turned on the television. From 9 a.m. onwards, I followed the cameras as each time zone ushered in the new millinnium. It was a moving experience, one that exuded a sense of hope and excitement.

Towards the end of 2000, I knew it was time to have a hip replacement. I had put the operation off for a few years, because I felt I was too young. For over two years, I had been using a stick when walking out of doors, which enabled me to walk faster, for longer periods, and with greater comfort. I am always amazed why people are so reluctant to use aids. My hip problem created mechanical difficulties, namely being unable to take full weight on that leg without discomfort. The answer was also a mechanical one: use a stick, so that some of the full weight on the bad hip can be transferred through the stick instead. Being elective surgery, and fortunately having VHI cover, I could choose the time and place I wanted, as well as the surgeon. Having worked with Jimmy Sheehan, and holding him in high regard, my preference was for him to do the job. I chose the end of November, as it suited me best from the garden perspective.

Fortunately, all went well. From the hospital, I went to a convalescent centre and, finally, to living independently at home, without any major hitches.

For some reason, the day before going into the hospital, I decided to bring my laptop. I have no idea why I did this. Then, two days later it occurred to me to write a diary about the experience as I was going through it, which I did, even on the day of the operation itself, as I had had an epidural injection instead of a full anaesthetic and so was alert from mid-afternoon on. In retrospect, I think writing the diary was a therapy in itself. After the first week, the notion came that I might try to publish these diaries, since my personal experience, coupled with my physiotherapy knowledge, might prove helpful to others. The diary covered six weeks: the first two weeks spent in the hospital, the second two weeks in a convalescent centre, and the third managing the first two weeks at home. I was encouraged to publish by Michael Garvey. His wife had had her surgery a year earlier and he had been looking for helpful literature and found none. So I went ahead, again using Eleona as the publishing name. The book's title is *Diary of a Hippy: Journeying through Surgery*. Jimmy Sheehan kindly launched the book, as well as allowing the use of the hospital's boardroom for the launch.

The day after that first three-month post-op period was over I was back working in Shekina. Indeed, that was the day I started digging out sods in the lawn to create Shekina's zen walk. This is designed in the form of a Celtic spiral, with a base of granite chips and a gingko tree in the centre. Many people seem to enjoy walking mindfully (hence slowly) along this pathway.

I knew after my first hip replacement that the other one also required attention. I was aware that Jimmy was to retire in the near future, so decided to have the second one done by him a year later. Again, I was grateful that all went well. This time, the post-op procedure differed in the sense that on my first hip, I was told to use two crutches for the first six weeks. On the second, I went onto one stick after one week. Otherwise the pattern was the same, with time spent convalescing before going home. Again, I do not know the origins of my inspiration, but during this period I wrote another book. The title speaks for itself – *Saying Yes to Life: A Way to Wisdom*. This book is more psychological, with chapters covering such topics as saying yes to personal existence, to otherness (people, the universe and time), and to the Ultimate Other. Tony Bates kindly agreed to write a few words for the back cover and John Quinn launched it.

Our Holy Land pilgrimages began to change in 1999. We went, as usual, in the spring of that year. I remember, on our visit to Bethlehem, the bus driver proudly showing us the enormous car park they had built for tour buses, in anticipation of the big crowds expected at Christmas that year – the 2000th anniversary of Jesus' birth. Alas, that was not to be. In the autumn of that year, the political scene deteriorated and we were unable to go, having been advised by the Department of Foreign Affairs. The Second Intifada started in September 2000, with mounting tension occurring in the months beforehand, and this meant we were unable to travel. In the autumn of 2001, Charlie and I went out to Israel to see the scene for ourselves, as we wanted to recommence our pilgrimages. Life was indeed quiet, with few pilgrims about. However, we felt it would be safe, but could see a change was needed regarding the places where we stayed. We were reluctant to leave the Holy Land East Hotel, but found the Ecce Homo Convent, which is within the walls of the Old City. They had fewer beds to offer, but we had already decided on taking smaller groups. Similarly, in Tiberias, we changed from the lovely Scotch Hospice, which was then being upgraded to a four-star hotel (and sadly in my estimation), leading to the centre losing its great charm. Instead, we opted for the Ron Beech, which was an Israeli family-run hotel. It was literally on the lakeshore, which made it attractive.

During this visit we rented a car, and I was amazed, as I drove from place to place, to discover how small the country actually is: the size of Munster (that is, before the Israelis started extending their settlements into Palestinian lands). Somehow, in a bus, and not driving oneself, it seemed larger. On this visit, we stayed in Ecce Homo in Jerusalem and in Galilee in the hostel of the Benedictine Monastery in Tabgha, a most beautiful spot, which includes within its grounds the area known as Dalmanutha.[67] It was good to return with a small group of fifteen the following year and this we continued to do annually up to the spring of 2006.

After the completion of my Master's in Theology in 1997, I continued to attend lectures and courses. Most courses were simply for personal faith enhancement, while two were helpful in the area of counselling and spiritual direction. For example, over the summers 1995–2003, I took part in one week of a three-week summer school run by the Redemptorists in Marianella. Two stood out – one on sexuality and spirituality given by a priest and sister from Canada (whose names I no longer remember), and the other a wonderful week with Con Casey, CSSR, on Christology. I attended other lectures, mainly chosen from the list of selected courses at the Milltown Institute. I recall three in particular, one on the theology of Hans Urs von Balthasar, given by Tom Dalzell SM (just two of us opted for this course), one by Finbarr Clancy s.j., on the Trinity, and one by Jack Finnegan SDB, on psychology and spirituality. Jack's course opened up for me the writings of Gerald May,[68] which impressed me enormously, especially his book *Will and Spirit*.

These courses prompted me to think of more serious study. The obvious route was to attempt a doctorate, but I was in my seventieth year! I thought the whole idea ridiculous at first, but the notion did not go away. I approached two of the Milltown Institute staff, who suggested I draft a rough proposal. Around the same time, the Time-Out Days in Shekina had become popular. I felt it would be good to reflect on what it was about the garden that seemed to nourish people in such a deeply spiritual and satisfying way. Then the penny dropped – why not research what was actually going on and do so under the direction of

---

[67] This spot is mentioned in Mark's Gospel: '[Jesus,] getting into the boat with his disciples, went to the region of Dalmanutha' (8:10). Dalmanutha is the name I gave to my home in Donnybrook. An Israeli guide explained the meaning of the word: 'manutha' referred to 'dwelling' and 'dal' to both the 'poor man' and the 'hospitable man'.

[68] May was a psychiatrist and a mystic. Just before he died, he published a book on mysticism.

an appointed supervisor, which a doctoral programme would offer?

I immediately outlined a loose proposal, which was rejected not for the proposal itself, but rather for the fact that I did not have a third language – even though the topic I was choosing did not require one. Rightly or wrongly, I had the feeling I was not wanted. This encounter was in complete contrast to the one I had with John Macken before my MA, and made me even more determined. I remember going home and phoning the postgraduate department at All Hallows. I was invited along, and because I had done my Masters by research and thesis, they accepted me there and then with no further questions, and with, at that stage, no proposal needed other than to give them a vague idea of the area I wished to explore. I was delighted and began my research there in the autumn of 2003.

I was fortunate, as I was with my MA, in being given Eugene Curran, SM, as my supervisor. I seemed to get off to a good start, as I had from the outset a relatively clear idea about how the thesis would evolve, unlike, it would seem, the other post-graduates starting off with me. Eugene gave me great freedom, helped to further my ideas, corrected me on others, and suggested reading material. I read copiously and was fortunate in being able to use the Milltown Park library, which is just up the road from my home. I kept solidly at it for two years. The part I really enjoyed was the thirteen in-depth interviews I had carried out with people who had participated in a Time-Out Day in Shekina the previous summer. These were recorded and then analysed.[69] I completed the work in November 2005 and had my defence in early December. This proved to be a memorable event in the sense that never before had I experienced myself being so confident in the academic world, both when presenting the thesis and when answering the examiners' questions and comments. What a relief and delight it was when, about half an hour later, I was told I had got my PhD. I should add here

---

[69] I used qualitative research methods for this thesis and analysed the data found in the transcripts under six themes. These themes linked in with the theoretical framework as set out in the first section of the thesis.

that the title of the thesis is 'Exploring Personal Experiences in a Garden in the Light of the Sacred'. I had my conferring the following March in the Helix Theatre, since Dublin City University were the conferring authority. My brother John came over for the day, he and Charlie filling my allowed allocation of two visitors. I still pinch myself when I see photos of myself in cap and gown, and even more so when I get the rare letter addressed to Dr Catherine McCann.

The thesis was over 200,000 words, so was quite a tome. I did not want the contents to remain hidden away in a college library and only in thesis form, since I felt large sections of it would be of interest to others. Fairly soon, and while my thoughts were fresh, I endeavoured to shorten and simplify the text into book form. I then started looking for a publisher. Following a few unsuccessful attempts I turned to the Paulist Press in America and they accepted it, much to my delight and gratitude. It was published under the title *New Paths toward the Sacred: Awakening the Awe Experience in Everyday Living*.

Throughout this period I continued counselling. Over the years, since my course in Tullabeg, I had a few clients for spiritual direction. In the early 2000s a new professional body was established, the AISGA (All-Ireland Spiritual Guidance Association). I was the first member to be accredited to this new association and renewed my affiliation until 2012. I had hoped this membership would have opened up more opportunities to work in this area but this did not materialise. I still counsel and spiritually direct a few clients, mostly people who had previously come to me and later wished to return for a few sessions, as well as the occasional new person.

Over the years, I have been asked to give the occasional spiritual talk to different groups. One I particularly remember was in Tralee, as part of a Lenten series of talks. I have forgotten my topic but know it had something to do with the importance of symbols, so I brought down some overheads of Shekina's sculptures to illustrate my talk. What I recall vividly was a remark by a lady during the Q&A, which delighted me: 'I never knew God was so big!' From the way she said it, I knew she had been graced by a major insight. I have also written the odd article for journals, and a lengthy chapter in *The Third Age Handbook*, edited by Anne Dempsey, entitled 'The Spiritual Dimension'. I was to use this later as a basis for several talks. But in the last few years, lecturing and writing just seemed to come to a natural end. Everything has its day: 'There is a time for everything …' (Ecclesiastes 3:1).

The prayer group meeting every Monday night has remained a constant event from its beginnings up to the present. I have only missed meetings on very rare occasions. Over the years, many members of the group have died, and while there have been new people, the numbers have gotten smaller. At the same time, the commitment of those who do come has become stronger and the bonds and friendships that exist within the group are remarkable. Music, in the form of hymn singing, is an important part of each meeting. Over previous decades we had guitar players, and when this ended I tried to step into the breach. I bought a digital piano that can play in organ mode, and this offers an adequate background to the singing. I sight-read music (poorly), but since much hymn music is only found in chords, this is the way I largely play. Sadly, or negligently, I never practise.

An important off-shoot of the prayer group that began around 2000 is the faith sharing group. This meets monthly and does just what the title says: share faith in as personal a way as possible. Those who come have found it extremely beneficial. We focus on a scriptural passage and each one shares personally on the meaning that passage has in their personal life story and particularly in their lives as lived today. Most in this group had been prepared for faith sharing by previously attending a course on Lectio Divina. Each of us looks forward to our faith sharing sessions, with few missing unless they absolutely have to. Another group, which we call the Iona group, was established some years after our visit there. This group meets more sporadically and comprises some of our group who visited Iona, as well as a group of Presbyterians who went around the same time as we did. It is a deeply ecumenical gathering and over the years we have drawn close to each other, especially in understanding and respecting each other's faith perspectives. There is little, in fact, that keeps us apart.

Other types of belongings of this period included my being invited onto two boards. The first of these was Aras Mhuire, the nursing home of the Medical Missionaries of Mary and the Kiltegan Fathers in Drogheda. I felt privileged to be asked and contributed as best I could as well as learning a great deal from this experience. I knew nothing before this about boards of management and their structure, nor did I realise the power and responsibility they have over organisations. Later I was invited to join the board of Maryville Nursing Home, just next door to me in Donnybrook. Again this was an enriching experience, blest with a very experienced chairman, but the board was unexpectedly disbanded when the Sisters of Charity decided to close down this nursing home.

An interest I started in the nineties was to return to where my apostolic spirit was born, namely the Gardiner Street and Seán MacDermott Street area of Dublin. I introduced myself to the parish priest and started going to Mass there on Wednesday mornings, after which I joined some of the women for a cuppa, as well as visiting a few families. I thought that might be a start but it did not lead to further developments. Sometime later, when the Salesian priests took over the parish, and not long after the parish councils started, I was asked by Michael Casey, the then parish priest, to become a member. I was delighted and was elected secretary. The life of this council had its ups and downs but I stayed on for several years, but eventually had to leave, finding it difficult to attend meetings. I also felt I had contributed what I could. I also attempted to establish a gathering for prayer in the heart of the city: in the middle of the day (lunchtime), in the middle of the week (Wednesdays) in the middle of the city (Dublin). This did not take off, so the idea had to be abandoned. I learned that unless one is gifted with a unique mission, most enterprises work through some kind of organisational framework.

Up to now, I have talked little about the primary group to which I belong, namely, the worldwide communion of the Catholic Church. Being part of it from four days after birth, it has over time become part of who I am. It is something deeper than being a member of or belonging to any other group, such as organisations or other gatherings. Rather it is a living reality into which we enter through baptism, thereby becoming members of Christ's body as well as being united with all who are baptised. The Church's life is based on Jesus' assurance: 'I am with you always; yes, to the end of time' (Matthew 28:20). The Church therefore contains immeasurable riches since the presence of divinity lies at its heart and is its raison d'être. But at the same time the Church is a human institution. Hence it has always been true that while we, the people of God, desire its riches and aspire towards holiness, at the same time as weak and vulnerable human beings we will always remain a community of sinners, a fact that some find hard to accept and especially in relation to its hierarchy – they too are also sinners.

My outward relationship with the Church is somewhat unusual, in the sense that I have never been a parish person. As a child I went to Mass either at the Poor Clares or in the convent chapel when at school, then later, as a religious, also in a convent chapel. When I left the sisters, I went to daily Masses in various places to suit my timetable. At weekends, I could be in Wicklow or Dublin, so again went to places that suited. I am more conscious of my being a member of the Church, perceived as a worldwide community of the disciples of Jesus, whose primary aim, like Jesus, is to set people free and to establish a more just world community. My experience of local community I find among family, friends and the various groups to which I belong, and most especially when a Eucharist is celebrated in these settings.

Before coming to recent good news about Church, some general comments are necessary. As in previous periods within the Church's history, the twenty-first century has for many (including myself at a certain level), been a distressing time. There have always been ups and downs in the Church's two millennia of history and so keeping a historical perspective on today's situation does help. Nevertheless, going from the highs of Vatican II in the 1960s to where Church life is today, particularly in Western culture, is an upsetting reality from my, and many of my friends', perspectives. The horrific nature of child abuse by clerics (while keeping in mind numbers are small) as well as the almost deeper upset due to the impoverished way Church authorities handled this situation cannot but have affected all of us who chose to remain within the Church. Until recently, many in positions of authority appeared to be more interested in protecting the Church's reputation than helping the abused children, as illustrated, for example, by their discouraging investigations by civil authorities. The way forward must be reversed, namely to regain a good reputation civil authority involvement is a must and certainly a must for anyone abused. Fortunately, the way this sad situation has been handled is much improved in relation to the Irish Church but does not seem to be the case in many other countries.

I have had first-hand knowledge through clients of those abused by clerics. It was deeply distressing hearing their stories, and I can only hope that facilitating them to talk and providing empathetic listening helped in some way. (All cases had previously been reported.) Dreadful as were these painful happenings, at no time have I felt drawn to leave the Church. In fact, I sense it would be almost impossible for me to do so, as it is part of who I am. Despite the shame I feel for these abuse atrocities and particularly by the way the hierarchical Church has responded, there has been alongside this awfulness a consistent witnessing to goodness and beauty through the Church's educational, medical, social, cultural and artistic contributions over centuries.[70] There has also been the amazing hidden and at times heroic lives lived by vast numbers of people throughout the world even to the point of persecution. Regarding the darker elements within Church life, my view is that when someone you love has sunk low, very low, that is the time to reach out in love all the more. I sense this would be Jesus' approach. He never showed approval for the sin, but he loved the sinner.

Other realities within the Church also bother me. Crucially, there appears to be, at both central and local levels of Church structures, failure to take on board the views of Vatican ll. This

---

[70] RTÉ's documentary *Lifers* aired in January 2013. It illustrates the amazing selfless work of three Irish missionaries living in three different countries.

has led, for instance, to the silencing of priests, not allowing open dialogue on theological matters and particularly around marriage difficulties and the whole area of sexuality in general. A more recent difficulty for me has been the way the new translation of the Mass was handled by the Vatican, as well as being upset by the translation itself. It has diminished for me and others the prayerfulness of the Eucharistic celebrations. In summary, I find the way the institutional Church expresses itself in such a centralist and authoritarian way to be a stumbling block that gets in the way of people discovering Jesus as shown us in the Gospels. 'Putting Jesus at the centre of Christianity'[71] must become the primary focus of the Church (be they hierarchy, religious or lay persons); everything else, e.g. structures, doctrines or practices, should flow from this core reality.

The scene has somewhat changed through the totally unexpected happening of Pope Benedict resigning and Pope Francis taking over. In my estimation this was and is good news. From his first homely words as he appeared on the balcony just after his election – 'Good evening' – followed by his asking the crowd on the square to pray for him, initiating a period of profound silence, hope sprang up in my heart and I felt we were on the cusp of something very new and very different. I have followed all that has been reported about his words and deeds and am filled with delight at all he has achieved so far. His words are simple, fresh, life-giving, apt, compassionate and Gospel-inspired. The list could go on. I immediately got a copy of his apostolic exhortation, *Evangelii Gaudium* (*The Joy of the Gospel*), and was heartened by all he said. Some say this gives a blueprint of his papacy. His great message of hope and mercy and avoidance of pre-judging people, no matter what irregular position they find themselves in, is something new in the last 200 years, certainly since Vatican I. Like many others I am attracted to his warm personality and particularly by his humility, sincerity, prayerfulness, lifestyle and genuine love of the poor, as well as the twinkle in his eye. It certainly increased my belief in the Holy Spirit's activity within the Church in the

---

[71] José Pagola, *Jesus: An Historical Approximation*, p. 445.

sense that the conclave of cardinals elected such a man of God. He 'speaks' often through his gestures and I mention two that touched me and which came early on in his papacy: first his washing of a Muslim girl's feet on Holy Thursday, and secondly the fact that his first trip outside Rome was to the small island of Lampedusa, where migrants from Africa struggle to get into Europe, and his saying Mass on a small boat in that harbour. I was impressed with the way for 40 minutes he fearlessly faced journalists' questions on his return flight from Brazil's youth gathering. Even the journalists were astounded, especially by his now much-quoted response to a question about homosexuals: 'Who am I to judge?' So if we have a leader like that, all that I said previously may in time be tackled, with much more besides being opened up for discussion. I am particularly interested in his wanting to become more united with the various Orthodox churches.

However, I am a realist, not an idealist and hence I know he has an enormous task ahead and particularly within the Church (and above all within the hierarchy), as he endeavours to hold together strong conservative and liberal wings. He certainly appears to want the Church to act in line with Vatican II, namely in a more collegial manner as shown by his move early on to set up a Council of Cardinals (eight men) with whom he meets regularly, as well as his recently forming a secretariat of bishops to prepare for the Synod on the Family. It all augers well, although parties on both sides of the divide will inevitably be disappointed. I have felt strongly over recent decades that many aspects of Church life have become obstacles rather than help to what is central within Christianity, namely Jesus, and how his story is presented to us through the Gospels. Francis seems to be restoring that focus.

In 2012, previous to Pope Francis's election, I was heartened when hearing a lecture given by Ladislas Orsy s.j. (mentioned in Chapter 8). He was very involved with the Vatican Council (he is now 93) yet he remains full of hope. His optimism springs from his awareness of the divine energy that is alive within the Church. He knew Pope John XXIII and spoke with love and tenderness about this great man and his vision for the Church.

A major council document echoes this vision, when it speaks of the Church wanting to move forward 'with joy and hope', embracing all peoples, and doing so by discerning 'the signs of the times'. Orsy was certainly being prophetic, as in less than a year Pope Francis was elected.

*****

I should also mention what being Irish means to me. The first time I became really aware of it and became fiercely patriotic was while at boarding school, especially on St Patrick's Day. In fact this simply meant the ten or so Irish girls wearing sham-rock, harps and other green, white and yellow ribbons or flags. The reaction to all of this by students and staff was to smile at it all. Some of the sisters had Irish backgrounds. Appreciation of my Irishness has grown considerably in the second half of life. Travelling around the country I am truly awestruck at the beauty of our landscape and over time, despite not knowing the language, my appreciation of our rich cultural heritage has also grown. These two factors came strikingly together on a magical visit to Skellig Michael while quite a storm was raging, so much so that the usual boat for taking visitors did not sail that day. I feel particularly blest having lived so much of my life in Dublin city with its wonderful location, having Dublin Bay on its east-ern boundary and mountains to the southwest. Special areas include our attractive Georgian architecture and squares, and particular spaces such as St Stephen's Green, College Green and the Phoenix Park. Of late we have the beautiful spire in our main thoroughfare, O'Connell Street, and many of the new buildings and bridges along the Liffey, including the Convention Centre and, not far away, Grand Canal Square.

However, I find recent negativities in Irish life disturbing. In the first decade after leaving the convent, the distinction between sacred and secular were largely intertwined. Secular realities such as work, rearing children, leisure activities and meeting friends make up most of our daily tasks and all of these have the possibility of alerting us to a sense of the sacred, as the poet Patrick Kavanagh well understood. The sacred is similarly connected with secular realities and especially for Christians since through the incarnation secularity has been assumed by Christ's humanity. However, the rise of secularism (note the negativity inherent in 'ism'), particularly in the Western world, has meant more people are less disposed towards discovering a sense of the sacred within their ordinary living. While respecting those who hold atheistic views, a large majority, as revealed in the last census, still claim a religious affiliation. Yet despite this fact, the media and also other influences such as philosophy and science have a tendency to support a world view that is solely empirically based, combined with an avoidance of raising pertinent 'why' questions. Secularism changes people's fundamental values and meanings. For instance, it can manifest itself in individualism, materialism, consumerism and personal 'fun' ('partying'), which become priorities in people's lives. For those caught up in this milieu, the sacred (or God) is less easily discerned, while for some it is definitely not wanted, and this fact can at times extend to the point of belittlement. I find this sad, and contrary to our Celtic tradition as well as the varying religious traditions that are still valued by many in our country today.

**

Various memorable family get-togethers have taken place over the decade. Brendan, my second nephew, married in Dublin in 2002, so all the troops gathered in Ireland for a few days for this event. Alan, my youngest nephew, married in New York in 2004 and all of us siblings went over to join in the celebration. Eoin, Alan's brother, married in Portland, USA, in 2009, and a month later they came over to have his Irish wedding party and chose Shekina as the venue. My sister Elizabeth celebrated her golden jubilee as a religious sister in 2006, and also had her party in Shekina. Apart from these celebrations, we siblings decided in the nineties to have a weekend away together. We chose the '0' dates, namely when John was 60, 70 and 80, while Monica, a decade younger, was 50, 60 and 70. On the first of these we went to Kerry, the second to Clare, and the third in 2013 in Maynooth (for my benefit as I did not want to be too far from Charlie on account of his recent fragile state).

From 2000 onwards, several grand-nephews and nieces arrived on the scene.[72] I now have six in the US: Mac, Henry, Declan, Nuala and Seamus; four in England: Jack, Ella, Orla and Greta; and three in Ireland: Lily May, Izzie and Melody. Since I do not remember, or even know, my nieces' and nephews' birthdays, I know with certitude that I would be the same with the next generation. Hence I decided to mark the birth of each arrival with a gift that might accrue a bit of wealth for each child over their first eighteen years. That is my thinking, and whether it works that way remains to be seen. While respecting their parents' wishes I am at the same time saddened that some of these children are not being familiarised with the Jesus story in their earlier years. I sometimes feel like saying to family, as well as to others, that the God you don't believe in I probably don't believe in either!

The last arrival, born 2 October 2012, in New York, necessitates more involvement on my part. The loveliest thing happened for me at the birth of this child: the parents (my nephew Jason and his wife Jessica) sent the usual email announcing the birth of the child with accompanying photos. Then, three days later, came another email to the family with the announcement: 'We have a name!' As it turned out they chose Charlie after my friend Charlie and explained why they had made this choice. In my email I received an additional request: would I be Charlie's spiritual mother? I was quite overwhelmed and of course said yes. Despite the big age gap I will do my best. They brought Charlie, at only two months old, to celebrate Christmas with us here in Dublin. It was touching to see Charlie senior (at 92), bless Charlie junior with Moses' lovely blessing: 'May the Lord bless you and keep you. May he let his face shine on you and be gracious to you. May he grant you his peace' (Numbers 6:24–26). The paparazzi were at work in the background to capture this special happening.

---

[72] See Appendix III for an overview of the family tree.

Friends have tended to remain in the background in this book. But they are there. I do not have numerous friends, as some people seem to have, but those I have I treasure, and they are good friends. Every year, just before Christmas, I gather together about eight women friends for lunch in my house in Dublin. My other usual form of meeting is for the occasional lunch. Muriel, whom I met through a carer group, has become a good friend and has been exceptionally kind in helping out with Toby and later Andy. In addition, many good friendships have grown from among people in the prayer group. My Christmas ritual is not complete without a visit to my oldest friend, Daphne. The same is true of Geraldine, but in Geraldine's case we meet more often. Over five summers at least, Charlie and I have had the joy of spending time with her on her boat, cruising on the Shannon as well as the canal.

I have been consistently modifying aspects of the garden in Shekina. Since 2000 I added six more sculptures, the last two being works in stainless steel by Michael Foley. The total number of sculptures is now eighteen. The cold period we had over Christmas 2010 led to the loss of some shrubs, so new planting was required. A major addition arrived in 2004. I had, over the years, some fairly large gatherings – one a sad one, to remember the death of Fred Conlon (two of his major works are in the garden). A big crowd came and it poured rain all day. It was difficult to fit them in the house and its small lean-to sunroom. In October of that year, I approached Seán Casey, head of the Parks and Wildlife South-Eastern Region, about building a larger sunroom. I did not know at the time he was about to retire, but he said he would look into the matter, and discovered some money that could be allocated to the project before the end of the year. In no time, the structure went up, built by Patrick Ward and his brother. He was an excellent builder and completed the work within the set timeframe. It is a wonderful addition to the place and transforms living there. It is a wraparound building extending over two sides of the house, so gives wonderful views of the garden, including being able to view ten of the sculptures. My job was to furnish it – blinds, rugs and of course furniture. I was fortunate enough, the summer before, to win a car in a local raffle supporting the Ballinacor Community Project. Instead of the car, I took the money and this covered all these expenses.

***

It is only when coming towards the end of my story that I realise that I have not mentioned an important area in my life: prayer. Maybe it is appropriate that it has worked out this way. I have referred to how celebrating daily Eucharist is a central focus in my life but said nothing about personal prayer. All prayer is based on having a personal relationship with God. Relationships can develop, if fostered, or fade away, and the same is true of those with God. For me this has meant that my understanding of God and the images and metaphors in relation to God that are meaningful to me have changed over the years, as well as the growing realisation that God is infinitely more in love with me than I can ever imagine. My understanding of God now is best described as 'Loving Mystery'[73] and this evolving sense of God as 'mystery that beckons' has meant my prayer life has also changed. Prayer, as I now perceive it, is essentially a movement into this mystery, a 'soaking in' of what God is.[74] Prayer is less about our effort and more about what we allow God do in us. This means letting the life of Jesus come alive in our life and especially during prayer. Authentic prayer must be in tune

---

[73] Herbert McCabe describes the term 'mystery' as 'the not-so-obvious, deeper meaning that is hidden at first … what shows itself but does not show itself easily. Mysteries are not for concealment but for revelation; it is because the revelation is so important and so profound that we have to work to understand it. As we understand mystery it enlarges our capacity for understanding' (*God Matters*, p. 76). He encourages us not to settle for superficial understandings, but to reach down in our attempts to understand life's deeper meanings and not settle for the merely scientific answer. Karl Rahner, one of the greatest theologians of the last century, and considered a mystic by many, placed 'the mystery we call God' at the centre of his vast range of writings. Experiencing mystery for him included an awareness of 'being addressed by what no longer has a name', the feeling of being 'protected by mystery', and a realisation that within this mystery lies 'the source of forgiveness, salvation and an eternal home' (*Practice of Faith*, pp. 52–53).

[74] I am indebted to Rowan Williams for two phrases in this sentence which articulate my thoughts in a very succinct manner. See *Being Christian* (2014).

with, as well as nourish, the way we live. The latter is beautifully summed up in one of my favourite scripture quotations:
'This is what the Lord asks of you: only this, to act justly, to love
tenderly and to walk humbly with your God' (Micah 6:8).

During religious life and for many years after leaving it, I
allocated daily time for personal prayer but less so in recent
years. Now my times of turning to God and allowing myself
be touched by his loving presence happen during ordinary
and sometimes unexpected moments throughout the day. That
turning is often spontaneous and centres sometimes on God
sensed as loving mystery; at other times on the Father to whom
I present myself, usually in a spirit of adoration; or on Jesus,
whom I know is with me and for whose companionship I am
deeply grateful; or on the Spirit, of whom I become conscious
in a variety of ways, in my breath, my energy and especially
when reaching out to others, when an insight emerges in connection with both secular and sacred realities, or when carrying
out automatic tasks such as mowing the grass, and especially
when exposed to beauty (Shekina, as a consequence, I find a
great help as a place of prayer). Over the years I am aware I
rarely turn to Mary, except when I find my emotions running
higher than normal and in a somewhat entangled fashion. I
sense as a woman she in some way could calm me down as well
as help me see through my feelings in clearer fashion. I have
little devotion to saints though I am an admirer of many, both
old and new.

At other times I find short aspirational prayers rising up from
within me. The most common one is 'Thank you Lord', which
can come on awakening in the morning, on being able to get out
of bed and do all the normal human tasks; it may arise through
someone's smile, sunshine appearing, or hearing about an incident on the radio. Literally, anything can become a trigger to
prayer. Other aspiration-type prayers I use tend to come from
the psalms: 'O God, you are my God' or 'O God, you are my
God for you I long' (Psalm 63). I discovered recently I could no
longer remember the Marian prayer, 'Hail, holy Queen', while
the act of contrition that I learned as a child is still rooted in my
memory: 'I love you Jesus my love, above all things. I repent

with my whole heart for having offended you. Never permit me to be separated from you and grant that I may love you always. Amen.' In fact, I rarely say formal prayers. On occasions I turn to two Ignatian ones: 'Take O Lord and receive …' and 'Dear Lord teach me to be generous …'. Neither do I pray 'for' people in a direct way, but rather, as St Paul says, I 'hold them in my heart' and sense that this moment or moments of awareness of others and their needs is prayer. I find prayers of petition difficult, and instead I use the formula where I state my concern, as shown in the Gospels by Mary, 'they have no wine' (John 2:3), or Martha, 'he whom you love is sick' (John 11:3).

I like to feel my day is punctuated with moments of being in God's presence. How this prayer 'works' is difficult to articulate and I am possibly foolish to try. I do believe that the prayer of being in God's presence is the simplest yet most profound form of prayer. Coming to a sense of the Divine presence within is faith's gift of a loving knowing which realises that God's presence is found within the depths of, or, alternatively put, as the ground of, our own personal awareness/consciousness. From an Ignatian perspective, 'finding God in all things' can become most profound when we give our full attention to God's presence, contented simply to be, aware simply that God is, is within our deepest selves, and allow ourselves to simply rest in him.

Frequently my reading can lead into prayerful moments, as can events, such as watching a television programme or a remark someone made in a conversation. I do set aside formal prayer times, just not as routinely as I previously did. My springboard to such prayer sometimes is a phrase from scripture, or doing a de Mello awareness exercise like listening to my breathing. During these prayer periods I often experience dryness, a sort of aridity. This does not upset me – many of the saints had a similar experience. However, it is great when gifted with moments of consolation; they do offer a great lift when they come. At the moment I value very much the prayers of the Mass, especially the four Eucharistic prayers and the prefaces of the various feasts and seasons. I more consciously attempt to enter and live in the spirit of the different seasons and feasts of the liturgical year. Some key texts of scripture are never far from consciousness, for example: 'I have loved you with an everlasting love' (Jeremiah 31:3); 'If only you knew what God is offering' (John 4:10); and 'I have come that they may have life and have it to the full' (John 10:10).

I would hope in the near future to return to saying the Office. Apart from its beautiful prayers I like it because I sense myself being united to the praying Church around the world, namely to the monastic orders as well as others who three times (some six times) a day recite the Office. Maybe too, in the future, I will return to giving more routine periods to daily prayer.

***

In the spring of 2006 we went to the Holy Land as usual, with a group of about fifteen. Sadly, just as we were completing the first week in Jerusalem, Charlie took ill rather dramatically as we were praying at the ninth station – Jesus' third fall. He had to be hospitalised and so could not continue the pilgrimage. Our agent in Israel got another guide, and fortunately we had a priest in the group, which meant the pilgrims' daily Mass would continue. Charlie's illness turned out to be serious and he was kept there for three weeks. He was in the Israeli Hadassah Hospital on the Mount of Olives. Palestinians also went to this hospital, and, as is customary with them, members of the family often stay at the bedside, including through the night. I decided to do likewise. Apart from wanting to do this, I had nowhere to stay, as the group had gone north. It was also difficult, from a security perspective, getting in and out of the hospital. Passport checking and questioning occurred each time. It was an anxious time and the medical personnel did not want him flying home until he had reached a certain level of wellness and then maintained it for a week. His Jesuit superiors at home were very supportive of me and, of course, concerned about Charlie and his care. Eventually, he was well enough to come home and the VHI were wonderful. They sent out a nurse to accompany him back to Dublin and only left him at the point when an ambulance was there to meet him at Dublin airport. He came to Shekina to convalesce before returning to his community in Campion House. He continued to improve, but from then on further pilgrimages were out of the question.

Life imperceptivity changed over the next seven years, as Charlie gradually needed more care. I was happy to do this. He stayed on in Campion for a year, coming down each weekend to Shekina. Then it was decided that nursing-home care was necessary. I was, fortunately, allowed to continue being involved in his care, such as getting him up in every morning, taking him out for a daily walk, a visit to my home each evening, seeing him into bed at night and then to Shekina every weekend. In the first couple of years he was still able to go, for instance, to the West to the lovely Lydon family in the Maam Cross area and also to Canterbury for Easter, where a memorable encounter took place. On leaving the cathedral in the snow after the Solemn Easter Sunday Eucharist, Charlie went up to Archbishop Rowan Williams and said 'I am a Jesuit priest. In the name of God what keeps us apart?' Williams tossed his head and then with a broad smile answered, 'Original sin I suppose!'

My choice was, and is, to continue looking after Charlie. This has meant letting go of certain things but I have been happy to do this. The great positive lies in the caring itself. It is just good to be there for him, as his physical and mental limitations became more pronounced. He can, and still does, say daily Mass and is always happy to celebrate it with other people. He is normally happy to meet people even if he does not always recognise them. Thank God, he has not lost his sense of humour. Most Monday nights he attends the prayer meeting and we all hang on the words he does share, due to the richness of its content. We are all astonished at the profundity and aliveness of his faith, combined with the simple way in which he can articulate his thoughts when speaking about God and Jesus. It is a time of blessing for all of us. I have been aware since I have known him how his presence in a room affects people. It is a serene presence and is often punctuated with joy as he attempts to lift people's spirits by a humorous comment.

Between caring activities I now have more time for reading, which includes the daily paper (*Irish Times*) and *The Tablet*, a weekly journal, which I read from cover to cover. The former keeps me in touch with Irish as well as world news and the latter with the universal Church and its various happenings around the world. When time permits, my book reading is largely of a theological nature. I watch more television than I used to, selecting my programmes for the week; it is great to be living in the age when we can record so easily. I have, in particular, seen more soccer and rugby matches than ever before. It has become pleasant sitting with Charlie watching these games before an open fire.

The future? It is in God's hands. I hope I can remain in receptive mode and at the same time be creative in whatever form that may express itself. My present situation has taught me to live more in the present, to take one day at a time, and even each moment of every day as it presents itself. It is a good way to live when I manage to do this. In some sense, I feel more inwardly alive and interested in what is happening in our world, in comparison with earlier years, when I was always on the go: constantly moving from a to b to c without leaving sufficient time for reflective pauses between activities. I have discovered that the spaces between a, b and c can be valuable, such as the spaces that occur daily as one activity ends and before the next begins. These spaces can all become rich moments of awareness and grace.

Epilogue

Winter 2013–2014

I bring my story to a close by summarising the salient elements that I feel influenced my perceptions on life, as well as the way I have actually lived out my human existence up to this moment in time. This personal history has revealed varying strands and I have presented these in a loose chronological manner. In this epilogue I give an overview of these strands under seven headings. From my perspective, I see these as seven great graces, or, more accurately, as seven gifts of the Spirit. Each named gift has enhanced my living with a great sense of abundance. I have titled this book *In Gratitude* because that expresses my deepest response to all I have received in life. I realise too, that having a sense of gratitude is itself a gift and that applies to life's ups as well as downs. All is a gift!

First Gift: Religious Faith

I have no doubt that my greatest grace has been the gift of religious faith, as experienced and lived within the Christian tradition. I simply cannot imagine what my life would be like without it. From earliest memories, up to today, my faith remains the backdrop to everything: it has been the source that gives meaning to my thinking and acts as an energiser in my loving and doing. It has gifted me with the knowing that God is, that God is love, and that God loved the world so much that he sent his Son, Jesus, who through his humanity enables us to perceive or intuit what a God of love is like in human terms. I treasure the church, which despite its many failings, has kept alive the Christian story, not only through the scriptures, but also through the richness of its tradition over two millennia.

In the midst of my often distracted form of living, I know, at a deeper level, that I am living in and having loving Mystery live within the depths of my being. This is what gives me a sense of aliveness in living, intellectually, emotionally and spiritually. Knowing too that this Mystery is imminent within everything that is created adds richness and beauty to living in our wonder-filled universe. Being gifted with treasures brings with it responsibility, and particularly the response to love one another, as well as the rest of creation. In addition, as a Christian, I am called to 'love one another as I have loved you' (John 15:12). This Jesus way of loving means reaching out to everybody, and especially those in great need.

One aspect of this gift is the inspiration it has given to try to embrace as fully as is possible each task that presents itself, be it, for example, dusting the stalls in Mount St Anne's convent chapel for two hours on a Saturday morning, serving in the Cappagh Hospital sweet shop, being present to patients and clients, attending to my studies, facilitating groups and pilgrims, or enjoying the company of friends. One of the most pleasurable activities in life is indeed good conversation. Echoes of my father's poem come to mind: 'If you have got a job to do, do it now.' More important has been Ignatius' words, 'finding God in all things' and particularly in 'the sacrament of the present moment' (de Caussade's phrase). De Caussade also said, 'the present moment contains more than we ever have the capacity to hold.' This I firmly believe and so riches are available to us in every moment of every day. That is where God's presence is found; the ordinariness of the activity in question matters little.[75] I like Hans Urs von Balthasar's words, where he says Jesus

---

[75] This is a form of 'mindful' living I have learned from Buddhist mindfulness, but for me this Christian way of living mindfully is richer since one discovers

never anticipated the will of his Father but received it moment by moment as it was given to him.[76] Another scripture passage lies deep in my awareness: 'to him whom much has been given, much is expected in return' (Luke 12:48). I certainly have been given much, but am aware also of the poverty of my response, and especially in the sense of 'what I have failed to do'. But even that knowledge is a further gift.

Second Gift: Charlie

From early on in our friendship, I saw this relationship as a great gift of God. Now, 43 years later, I see this even more so, and as with all the six gifts I mention, I am filled with gratitude. In the early days of the relationship, we obviously fell in love. How long this lasted I am not sure, but it did move fairly early on to the 'being in love' stage, which has lasted all these years. I would describe it as a deeply intimate relationship. I recall a homily Charlie gave at my sister's wedding where he said we cannot choose to sleep, we just fall into it, and similarly we cannot choose to fall in love, it just happens. We can, however, choose how we live out this love, and our choice was to allow gestures of affection without having full sexual expression. Throughout our friendship, I have always known Charlie to be committed to his Jesuit vocation, while at the same time being supportive of me and a great encourager in all my endeavours.

As is shown in my story, many of the happenings of my life in regard to the groups we set up, or the pilgrimages we initiated and led, were joint ventures. Neither of us could have done it alone. Family and friends were also shared. In recent years I am now sharing in Charlie's care and trust that I will be able to do what Jesus did, namely, 'love [him] to the end' (John 13:1). He still is able to say Mass, although at times I am the only member of the congregation. Here I am blest to receive his unique gift, not only of saying slowly a prayerful Mass, but also offering a life-giving word on the Gospel of the day. His more recent

---

'Presence' at its core.

[76] See his *A Theology of History* (1963).

prayer group sharings reveal above all the simple profundity of his faith, which he is able to articulate in a way that enhances everyone. As one of his Jesuit companions, a theologian, said, he has a deep grasp of theology. This knowledge is enriched further by his great love of the Gospels. Being close to someone who lives out of this richness is indeed a great grace.

Third Gift: Family and Friends

The first two decades of my life were intertwined with the lives of my brother and sisters so I owe each of them a deep sense of gratitude, and especially my brother, John, who influenced my life greatly. As we went our various ways, we have always kept in contact. Now that we are in the digital age, contact for some has moved towards emails and Skype. I do not use the latter and am not a great user of emails. I still prefer the phone, where you hear the human voice and the contact is immediate. My nieces and nephews I know, but some grand-nieces and nephews I have yet to see. I imagine little personalities emerging as I view their photographs.

I have been friendly with many people over the years – in childhood, in religious life, in student and work situations, etc. There are of course degrees of friendship and many have slipped out of sight as situations change. I do, fortunately, have a small group of friends who I know are always there for me and I hope they know I am there for them. Three have sadly died: Marie Webb, Sr Bride and Sr Alphonsus. There are always the faithful group of 'rememberers' who send cards at Christmas and it is always good to receive these.

Fourth Gift: Shekina

I constantly am amazed at the great gift Shekina has been in my life. My appreciation and love of the place, combined with my awesome sense of the beauty that the garden and its surroundings offer, never fails to nourish and delight me. That part of this beauty is the work of human hands (including my own) adds to my astonishment when I allow its beauty to enfold and caress me. I know visitors are captured, often instantly, by both the beauty and peace of Shekina, and often want to linger in its various seating areas, and for some this has meant lying flat out on the lawn. That my gift of the place to the nation was accepted gives me added pleasure and gratitude, in the sense that I know this is to continue as a sculpture garden. I would find it very difficult to hand over the garden if, for example, ill health incapacitated me, but knowing that I have to leave in the Lord's hands. My relationship with Shekina has changed over the years. I first viewed myself as gardener, then more as caretaker[77] and of late as curator; in truth it is a mixture of all three. In the recent past I have begun to see that my second 'call', or 'call within a call' to 'come to a land that I will show you' (Genesis 12:1) is being answered, with Shekina being that 'land'.

Fifth Gift: Patients, Clients, Workshop Participants

I sometimes wonder in amazement at the large number of patients I have treated over the years, in St Anthony's Rehabilitation Centre, Cappagh Hospital and Baggot Street Hospital. It would certainly run into many thousands. Whatever way I helped them, I know the return they gave me was great. How true that 'in giving we receive'. The patient–therapist relationship can become close, in particular with those suffering from long-term conditions. I can still recall with deep affection some of these people, including, at times, their families.

Regarding clients, I have always felt enriched by the way people share their story, especially its difficult, maybe even darker, side. Attempting to accompany them as they struggle to find a solution, or at least a better way to manage their problems, is humbling. I have indeed learned much about human living from listening to clients. As a consequence, I have been gifted with a broader and more empathetic view on people's

---

[77] Caretaker in the sense of Adam and Eve's primary role being 'to cultivate and take care of it [the garden of Eden]' (Genesis 2:15).

lives. This view helps prevent rushing to judgement in regard to how people think and behave the way they do.

I am grateful to the many people who came to my workshops and for the interest and appreciation they showed. I benefited also from their responses, which enabled me to modify what I offered. I was aware at the time of the trust placed in me by those who organised such events. I usually felt excited before each workshop began, and grateful at the end that people felt satisfied, even enriched.

Sixth Gift: Holy Land and Other Pilgrimages

Over the years Charlie and I took more than 1,000 people on our 40 pilgrimages to the Holy Land. As well as exposing our groups to the history, culture, religions and, of course, the geography of the country, our main purpose was to afford pilgrims an opportunity to answer the question that Jesus put to his disciples: 'Who do you say that I am?' When in the Holy Land, the humanity of Jesus comes strongly to the fore and people frequently grow in their intimacy with him precisely because of this new knowledge. The impact on my own faith over the 40 times I visited was inevitably great, although hard to put into words. Scripture, and in particular the Gospels, came alive in a new way, and each year more so. It was like a drip feed, twice yearly, nourishing my faith. I also saw these pilgrimages as an apostolate, and what joy it brought when, so many times, we witnessed our pilgrims having their eyes opened to receive a deeper glimpse as to who Jesus was and is for us today when we allow his presence to enter more fully into our lives. Years later I sometimes meet people who came on pilgrimage with us who speak of how transforming this event was in their life.

Seventh Gift: Books and Theses

To discover, in my later years, that I had the gift of writing was a humbling yet exciting experience. When writing, I was aware of those who would actually read the book. This gave me a kind of hidden bond with readers. I owe a debt of gratitude to those who did read, and who seemed to benefit from, what I wrote. It meant sales, but more importantly it affirmed that what I wrote was of value to readers and this in turn gave me confidence to write the next book. I was indeed grateful to publishers who put their trust in me, and, regarding the self-published works, to their designers and printers. This present book is my seventh – the seventh of gift number seven.

When I think of my studies and theses in particular, how grateful I am for the many wonderful opportunities that I have had in the pursuit of further knowledge: Rome, Milltown Park, All Hallows, and, before that, my physiotherapy studies. Many, I realise, are not so fortunate. I cannot imagine now what my life would be like without these blessings.

***

My motivation in writing this work evolved as I wrote, without becoming crystal clear. A reason from the start, and one which has persisted during writing, is simply being drawn to carrying out this task. I do not see it as personal therapy. People write autobiographies, I imagine, for many reasons. Several come from people who are famous, others because they have a tragic story to tell, or those, due to their bravery, who have worked through something, be it illness or an adventure. Mine, apart from the earlier years, has been ordinary enough, although undoubtedly it has been gifted with many opportunities. I believe there is value in the ordinary, and recording that ordinary just as it occurred. Hence, I hope those who choose to read this book will be alerted to valuing their own story with whatever ups and downs it contains.

Final thoughts: We can give away wealth in the form of money or goods or by freely sharing our talents. Our most personal possession is our story. Is there value in sharing it with others? Views on this would, I imagine, vary. One of my core beliefs is the value of every human being, a fact which necessitates valuing each person's story. Valuing is, I realise, one thing but sharing it is another. I do not think it is pride that prompts me. Adding to the bank of history, yes, but is there some other

Matilda – Old London taxi

*Elizabeth (Sr Madeleine) and Catherine
(Sr Paul Mary)*

*Catherine and Charlie
in the Holy Land*

John and Catherine

Catherine (age 15)

McCann children – Monica, Bridget, Elizabeth, Catherine and John

Drawing rooms

My father – John McCann   *My mother – Madeleine McCann*

Front view of Simmonscourt

Side view of Simmonscourt

Pond in Shekina

Michael D. Higgins in Shekina on the day of the handover to the State

Gazebo and two sculptures (by Alexandria Wejchert and Michael Casey), Shekina

My first sculpture,
by Cliodna Cussen

Andy

Charlie and Catherine

Catherine presents her first book to President Mary Robinson

John, Bridget, Monica, Elizabeth and Catherine

Dr Catherine with Charlie and John

motivation? If pushed, I would say sharing what I have been gifted with in life is an important reason and linked with this is my desire to say thanks to all the people who have touched my life.

Ultimately, the most likely reason for sharing this story has to do with my religious faith and the incredible enriched dimension to living that it has given. Feeling drawn to tell others about the central role faith has played in my life was confirmed on hearing how the new understanding of evangelising has moved from the traditional form of sending missioners abroad to individuals sharing their personal faith experiences where they live. My faith has been a thread running through my life. I have truthfully experienced it to be what it proclaims: Good News! Indeed, very Good News and news that is available to everyone:

'From his fullness we have all received, grace upon grace' (John 1:16).

Postscript

Charlie died 3 February 2014.

'No one can snatch him
Out of the Father's care'
John 10:29

***

Happily I read to Charlie the entire contents of this book before he died. He gave his approval, suggesting the odd change of word. I experienced this as a blessing; a blessing which gave me the assurance to seek a publisher. I am now grateful to Orpen Press for accepting this work.

APPENDIX I

Outline of the Grounds Made from Personal Memory

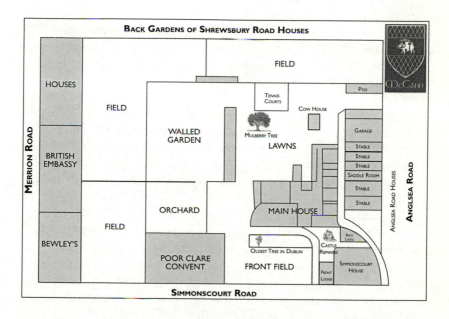

The grounds incorporated a garden area, although the majority of the land was really a mini-farm. What an extraordinary richness this provided for my siblings and me to have the experience of farm life while being part of city living. The farm had four large fields, one in the front and three at the back and side of the house, for the cows and horses. There were normally about five milking cows and a calf appeared occasionally. This meant fresh milk every day, often hot from the cow with the froth on top. I did try to learn to milk, but not very satisfactorily. There was a man who looked after the cows as well as helping in the grounds. I had my own pony and there were other horses: my father, a keen horseman, kept his hunters at a farm he owned in Ratoath, County Meath, but the polo ponies were cared for in the stables at Simmonscourt and sometimes brought to Sandymount Strand for their exercise. I recall a saddle room and a stable sectioned to house three horses with a hay loft above, and three other single stables.

A piggery, housing around six pigs at a time, and a sizeable hen house were located down among the fields, which meant that fresh eggs were always available. A few turkeys appeared coming up to Christmas, and for a short while we had ducks. Of interest was the area for the rabbits, since I was the owner of two of these for a couple of years and hence became responsible for their wellbeing. My mother was particularly fond of dogs. We had several family dogs over the years, including a Pekinese, a Dalmatian and a spaniel. The place was so large that several strayed, never to be seen again.

In line with the stables was a garage with room for three cars. Also in the backyard area was a well, which we called the pump. From it we were able to have delicious water, which completely spoilt my taste for tap water once I had left home. Opposite this well and making up part of the house was the boiler, which heated the downstairs of the house and, even then, only the main rooms. The upstairs bedrooms had mostly fireplaces, many of which were converted into gas fires in my lifetime.

The gardens were further subdivided, with a wide stretch of grass around the house that we used as a croquet lawn, a place for clock golf and even a miniature nine-hole golf course. In the centre of one part of the lawn stood a huge mulberry tree with two other trees nearby, favourites for hanging swings and a rope. We played a lot of tennis on the three tennis courts, two grass and one hard. Two summer houses stood here, one of which could be rotated.

Behind the lawn area was a long grass walk with a sundial in the middle and herbaceous borders to either side. Beyond these borders on both sides was the orchard. It was divided up into sections, with path intersections all lined with box hedging. The fruits included apple, pear, cherry and plum trees as well as gooseberry bushes and white and redcurrant bushes. Peach and nectarine trees grew against the walls surrounding three sides of the orchard – how lovely it was to pick and eat a peach warmed by the sunshine. Vegetables and soft fruits grew in the large walled garden, which contained one big and two smaller greenhouses. Grape vines, one black and one white, were planted in two sections of the large greenhouse. There was also a fig tree and areas for seedlings and cuttings as well as for more fragile flowers such as carnations. Having all this fruit and vegetables meant there was an ample amount to feed the household.

On the front lawn were two magnificent specimen trees, a large weeping willow and a *Taxus baccata*, or common yew. The latter now has a preservation order on it from the Tree Council of Ireland, stating it is the oldest tree in Dublin, at around 250 years old. Sadly the weeping willow is no more. When I pulled back my curtains each morning and saw the yew little did I know I was looking at such an ancient tree. Another area that deserves mention is the two shrubberies. The smaller front one, which surrounded two sides of the front field, gave a pathway to a private side entrance to the Poor Clare Convent. The larger shrubbery contained a pathway, often partially overgrown, which formed the boundary around the two large back fields. There were two lodges: the front lodge, where the head gardener lived, and the back lodge, which was the home of the butler and his family. Describing it now, it sounds very much like a paradise, as indeed it was.

Appendix II

Plan of the Inside of Simmonscourt
Made from Personal Memory

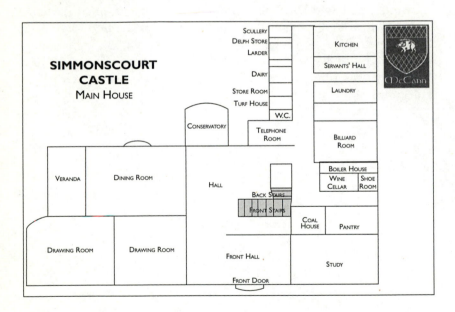

The main elegant and spacious ground floor rooms were comprised of a front and main hall, a double drawing room (the first with lovely plaster work and parquet floor used solely for entertaining), dining room with adjoining veranda (used for breakfast and lunch in the summer months), the study (given to John and me as 'our room' in our teen years and where he began his great classical record/CD collection) and a conservatory always stocked with a variety of plants changed every season.

At the end of the hall was the telephone room which also contained all the gaming equipment: tennis racquets, golf clubs, fishing rods and my father's guns for his shooting expeditions down the country. Outside this room was an intersection between the long and shorter ends of a corridor. At this intersection, there was a large press called, quaintly, the 'set-off'. Food was brought here from the kitchen and relayed to the dining room by the butler and parlour maid. Off the shorter corridor were the pantry, where all the delft and glassware was kept and the washing up and cleaning of the silver and brassware was done, the shoe room and a cellar for wines, spirits and liqueurs.

Down the longer corridor, there was a large room known as the billiard room. This was used as our sitting room and a fire was always lit in wintertime. Farther along were the servants'[78] quarters, their dining room, five bedrooms and a bathroom, as well as a laundry room, a store room, the dairy where the milk was separated and sometimes cheese was made, larder, large kitchen, scullery and a room containing the dinner services.

The upper floor of the front area of the house had different levels. There was the nursery area, containing a day and night nursery and a bathroom with a storey above with two bedrooms and the oratory. Continuing up the main staircase led to our parents' bedroom, off which was my father's dressing room. All along the front of the house were four large-sized bedrooms, three doubles and one single, and just one bathroom and toilet.

Although the house was big, it had a comfortable feel and a sense of being well lived in. The drawing room had some of the best furniture, the special china ornaments and a grand piano. The dining room contained most of the silver – a lot of it old Irish pieces, which my father collected. There were pictures everywhere. None of these impressed me in a notable way, but I did like several because of their lovely gilt frames. In particular I appreciated some of the fireplaces, clocks, lamps and Persian rugs. Above all I liked the lovely furniture – bookcases, sideboards, cabinets, chests of drawers, chairs, sofas,

---

[78] Unlike *Downton Abbey*, ours was not an upstairs–downstairs set-up but rather a north–south divide. Neither did it have anything like the grandeur of that setting, lest the reader be led astray.

tables. Many items were made of satinwood, often inlaid. The others were largely mahogany. My father at times commissioned pieces from Hicks, the famous Irish furniture maker. A unique piece of furniture was our mahogany dining-room table. It was normally set to seat eight people, but it could be extended twice by putting in extra leaves to seat twelve or sixteen and still remain round.